Covenant Keeping

BUILDING RELATIONSHIPS
THAT LAST

BY JIM DIPALMA

Dedication

I dedicate this book to my daughter Rebecka, my daughter Janelle and my son James-David. You are very special to me, and I thank God for you. I love you so much.

To World Overcomers Church:

I am so blessed to be your Pastor. You are a Revolutionary, Radical Remnant people, appointed by God for such a time as this, choosing to stay on course for the fulfillment of your destiny. You truly are World Overcomers and Covenant Keepers. I encourage you to keep walking in the fear of the Lord, and you will find great favor with God and man. As far as I'm concerned, you are the best in the Midwest and anywhere else.

To Every Five-Fold Ministry Gift:

You are truly gifts to the body of Christ. Your labor of love is greatly appreciated even when it seems like it's not. I want to encourage you, your spouse and children — don't give up, don't quit, we need you. Remember, in the end, it will all be worth it, for the prize is always greater than the price.

And finally, this book is dedicated to everyone bold enough, unselfish enough, willing enough, humble enough and loving enough to do whatever it takes to be committed and submitted to the entire counsel of the covenant of The Word of God.

In Memory of:

My mom, Julie, who's great legacy continues to challenge me to go further and deeper in the Lord.

Acknowledgment:

To Ed Bisconti, I appreciate you so much for taking the time and helping with the proof of the manuscript. You are a great blessing. Thank You.

To David and Linda Zidek, for your assistance in enabling the vision of this book to come to pass. Thanks a million.

To Lance Kupisch, for all of the advice you have given in making this book go forward. I appreciate you.

Foreword

During the stormiest season of my life and ministry, I met Pastor Jim DiPalma when he invited me to minister at his church. We quickly became close friends and I also bonded with his lovely wife, Joni and their children.

In the next few years I was besieged in my ministry through escalating lease payments ($64,000 per month), a war with my city to obtain use permits (over five years), the departure of my congregation (including my board of directors), malicious false accusations against my character, and near bankruptcy.

Many of my ministry friends and associates distanced themselves from me to observe whether I would survive or not. Some even prophesied my ultimate failure.

But Jim and Joni stood by me, invited me to minister, and showed me loving honor no matter what men said or thought.

Proverbs 20:6 says, "Most men will proclaim each his own goodness, but who can find a faithful man?" That word faithful in the Hebrew means "a loyal covenant-keeping person." Jim and Joni DiPalma stayed in an unconditional loving relationship with me in spite of my flaws, lack of popularity and the impending disaster bearing down on me. Today I am blessed in every way.

God hates covenant-breaking and looks for a new order of Christians who won't even break covenant with those who betray them, speak evil of them, and fall back into worldly bondage.

The Lord is married to the backslider (Jeremiah 3:14), and we should follow His example. In this book, **Covenant Keeping:** *Building Relationships That Last,* Jim DiPalma takes you on an exciting Biblical journey through the stages and blessings which will finally mature the church and prepare her for God's last days visitation.

I hope you are as blessed as I have been to discover the principles of covenant keeping!

Dr. Gary Greenwald
Senior Pastor, Eagle's Nest Ministries
Irvine, California

Table of Contents

Introduction

Covenant Keeping

I believe that this message on covenant keeping is the most important message of my life and ministry. God has brought me to this point for such a time as this, so that I might declare fully the message of how to keep covenant.

My understanding of covenant comes not from the shallow seeds of human wisdom, but the generational heritage that has been laid up for me by my predecessors. I am a third generation Christian, raised in a godly home, surrounded by godly men and women who knew how to walk in covenant with God and one another. I learned how to keep covenant at a very early age through these faithful men and women of God. Through their lives, God taught me what I now know about covenant keeping. I have seen these godly men and women keep their covenant with God and godly covenants with others in spite of the difficult circumstances they were experiencing. I am a living testimony to their faithfulness as men and women of covenant. I have witnessed, through their example, the spiritual power resident in keeping covenant. This is why I am now able to declare to you this awesome truth about covenant keeping.

My desire in writing this book is to help you understand that we are living in the greatest hour in the history of the church. We are among the generation of those who will seek to not only make covenant with God and one another, but to keep it. God, through us, will raise up a glorious, victorious, overcoming church. This is what we were created for, and this is why the river of revival is flowing throughout the church worldwide. God desires to sweep the nations into His presence. This will require us to be in a place of genuine covenantal relationships, for it is here where the holy presence of God flows freely. Psalm 133 says,

> *"Behold how good and pleasant it is for brethren to dwell together in unity! It's like the precious ointment upon the head that ran down upon the beard even Aaron's beard: that went down to his garments; as the dew of Hermon, and as the dew that descended upon the mountains of Zion: for there the Lord commanded the blessing, even life for evermore."*

What a perfect picture of covenant! This is what true covenant keepers experience day in and day out. The place of covenant is a place of continual blessing and anointing. Praise God!

Called to Covenant

We were made to be in covenant with God and each other. The desire to be in covenant has been put into the heart of every man, woman and child. This is the reason we will often go through life dissatisfied by the casual relationships offered to us by the world — we want something more. We want relationships built upon committed covenantal love, rather than a life filled with casual, convenient love. This is why those who live in the fast lane often find that they are going nowhere fast.

Genuine love cannot be found where there is no commitment, for commitment is the foundation upon which relationships are built. Our relationships are only as strong as our commitment to them. For this reason, the enemy has sought to sow seeds of destruction into marriages, families, churches and businesses through a misguided understanding of covenant. The devil wants us to be like him, a covenant breaker, so he can rob us of the authority that God has given us through covenant and the devil knows that if he can keep us ignorant of the importance of keeping covenant, then we will more than likely break it.

Breaking covenant is a serious thing in the sight of God. God does not like it when we break our covenant with Him or godly covenants with others. God is jealous over the issue of covenant: He knows that when we break covenant with Him, or one another, in our marriage, family, church or business, we are fast on our way to a fall. When we break covenant with God or godly covenants with others, we are sowing seeds of destruction into our lives that will cause us to reap a bitter harvest. This is why we, as a nation, have fallen to the point we are at today — we have broken our covenant with God and godly covenants with one another.

We, as a nation, have misunderstood the importance of covenant keeping.This is why we have not placed a high value on the covenants we have made with God and each other. We have, through our own ignorance, taken upon ourselves the attitude of the covenant breaker, which is, "my kingdom come, my will be done." This is why we, as a nation, are right now tasting the bitter fruit of the curse associated with breaking godly covenant, instead of experiencing the blessing associated with keeping it. Isn't it time that we repent for breaking covenant, individually, and as a nation? The time has come for us to say the words our Father in heaven longs to hear, *"Your kingdom come, Your will be done, on earth, as it is in heaven" (Luke 11:2)*.

This is the place our Father longs to bring us: His will being done in our lives on earth, as it is in heaven. Why then can it often seem like we are experiencing hell on earth? Because we often pursue God's will, our way. We cannot use the flesh to defeat the flesh. The only way that we can hope to walk in the will of God is by the Spirit. Jesus said, *"It is the Spirit that gives life; the flesh profits nothing" (John 6:63)*. Jesus was telling us that the only way to walk according to the will of God is by the Spirit. This is why we must lay aside our earthly plans and agendas. They will prevent us from keeping our covenant with God and godly covenants with others.

The flesh cannot help us keep the godly covenants in our lives. When we try to keep a godly covenant our way, we will eventually fail. It is impossible for the flesh to aid us in keeping a covenant established by the Holy Spirit in our lives. It takes the power of the Holy Spirit working in our lives to keep a covenant established by Him. This is why Jesus told us, *"The words that I speak to you are Spirit and they are life" (John 6:63)*.

The Word of God, which is Spirit, has been given to help us keep the godly covenants established in our lives by the Holy Spirit. This is why we must lay aside our own thoughts and agendas — they will not help us keep the godly covenants in

3

our lives. The only way to keep the godly covenants established in our lives is by doing it God's way. We will never be able to keep a godly covenant our way, for our fleshly attempts to do something of the Spirit will always fail. This is why so many of us have failed to keep the godly covenants established in our lives: We have tried to do it our way, according to the flesh. This is why we must lay aside the imaginations of our own minds and pick up the Word of God. God's Word is what will help us keep the godly covenants we have made, and keep us from falling into the pitfall of our own opinions.

Connection Brings Protection

It is time for us to come to a place of maturity in our relationships. We should no longer base our covenant with God and godly covenants with others upon our own thoughts, feelings, opinions or imaginations. We must stop being offended by others just because we don't agree with them over particular issues. Too many Christians are willing to end relationships, and break godly covenant, over minor issues. We have majored on minors for far too long and as a result, have lost sight of a very important Biblical truth — covenant keeping. Our ability to keep covenant is of major importance to God, and goes way beyond our ability to agree with one another. We can disagree with one another and still keep covenant. Our being in covenant is not based upon us being in agreement. Covenant is an agreement that we make before God in the sight of God. This is the foundation upon which genuine covenant is built.

Covenant is a choice. I have chosen to be in covenant with my wife Joni. On May 10th, 1986, we made a covenant that we will not break! Our covenant of marriage is not based upon us being in agreement over particular issues. Just because I may disagree with her, or she may disagree with me, over a particular issue happening in our lives, does not give us the right to break our marriage covenant with each other. It is this ability to remain in covenant, in spite of our disagreements, that has strengthened our marriage and brought us to a place of deeper intimacy. We know that we can genuinely be honest with one another without fear of divorce. It is this trust in our marriage covenant that has enabled us to enter into the blessing and power that genuine covenant brings.

Covenant brings with it blessing. Through covenant, connection brings protection. God's favor rests upon those who keep their covenant with Him and godly covenants with others. God has poured out tremendous blessings upon me, and done wondrous things in my life, because I have kept covenant with Him and those that He has placed in my life. By the grace of God, I am a living example of what God can do in the life of someone who is willing to become a covenant keeper. I cannot even begin to imagine what my life would be like today if I had not learned what the Bible says about covenant keeping. Yet there is one thing that I do know, my life would be very different from what it is today. I know there is no way I would have received or enjoyed the incredible blessings God has given me if I had not received this revelation of covenant keeping. I would truly be a lost man without this piece of powerful practical wisdom from God.

There are many of you who desire the blessing of God upon your life, but I want to ask you: Are you willing to become a covenant keeper? Are you willing to allow the Lord Jesus to become the Lord of your relationships? I can tell you from my own experience that there are tremendous blessings awaiting those who make Jesus Lord of their relationships. I have personally experienced the blessing of making Jesus Lord of my relationships.

From the time when I, as a child, was pastored and mentored by Robert Burgess *(Robert Burgess has since gone on to be with the Lord)*, a genuine man of God who by his example taught me the value of maintaining an attitude of integrity and unconditional love, till now, my relationships have been blessed by God. Not that it hasn't taken a lot of work, it has. I have had to learn, through experience, the things that I am writing in this book. I have been deeply hurt by people who were not committed to keeping covenant with me. My understanding of covenant keeping goes way beyond head knowledge to actual experience; I know the power of God resident in keeping covenant. This is what I want to impart to you through this book — my understanding of covenant keeping.

I want you to experience the power and blessing of being in committed covenantal relationships as I have. There are many things that I have learned about keeping covenant that I will share with you in this book. These truths will help you learn about covenant so that you can keep covenant with God and godly covenants with others. You will learn what covenant is, who to make covenant with and how to keep covenant.

So often when I begin talking about covenant with believers, they start thinking about blood covenant. And, while the blood covenant we have through Jesus Christ is vitally important, covenant is more than this. We have so much more available to us through covenant than we have imagined.

One of my favorite verses, Ephesians 3:20, a verse that I think about often, says,

"Now unto Him that is able to do exceedingly abundantly above all that we ask or think according to the power that works in us."

This verse is special to me, for I have seen it at work in my life. From the time I received and began walking in this revelation of covenant keeping, this verse has become real to me. I know that I serve a big God, a God who is bigger than anything I can imagine Him to be.

You Can Keep Covenant

God is bigger than any relationship problems we may have in our lives. God is able to deliver us from the things that hinder and keep us from entering into long-lasting relationships. We can have relationships that are built upon the rock solid foundation of Christ. God desires for us to have these types of relationships in our lives. And, though our relationships may be challenged, tested, tempted and tried, God will cause us to come out on top, if we remain committed to keeping covenant. This is why I want to encourage you by saying what Michael W. Smith sings, which is, *"friends, are truly friends forever, if the Lord is the Lord of them."*

We can have confidence and hope from God, even in the face of adversity, especially in the area of our relationships. God is not shaken by our relationship problems, but moved with the feelings of our infirmities in the midst of them. God is able to save us from every relationship problem when we put our trust in Him. This is why keeping covenant with God and godly covenants with others is so important — it is a powerful act of faith that shows us our trust is truly in God, not ourselves or others.

Covenant was never intended by God to bring us into bondage. Under no circumstances should we allow ourselves to be brought into bondage through a false pretense of keeping covenant. Many people fear entering into covenant because they have been hurt at one time or another by someone who didn't keep covenant. They fear that they will be controlled, manipulated or dominated by another person under the appearance of covenant. This is not a godly view of covenant, but an ungodly one.

Godly covenant is a blessing; this is what God intended it to be. When we enter into godly covenants with others, our lives will be blessed through these covenants. What are godly covenants? They are covenants established by the Holy Spirit in our lives. Those who keep this kind of covenant will be blessed by God through it.

Yet, there are ungodly covenants that we can get trapped in and not even realize it. These covenants can become fleshly, lustful and even demonic. We can be led astray, even departing from the Lord, if we don't keep ourselves pure in the area of covenant keeping. Making covenant with someone is a serious decision and should not be treated lightly. Our covenants with others are serious business, for they have the ability to affect every area of our life.

I am amazed by casual view we often take of our relationships with others. I have found that people will often enter into covenant with others without the guidance of the Holy Spirit. As a result, these individuals will often cater to their flesh, through lust, rather than being led by the Holy Spirit into godly relationships. When we enter into covenant this way, it is ungodly.

This is one of the main reasons we have so many broken covenants in the church. We have made covenants the world's way and, as a result, have reaped a whirlwind of divorce and division. This is why we need to hear not only what covenant is and how to keep it, but more importantly, when and when not to make covenant.

There are times when we should not make covenant with people. Not every person that I meet is a candidate for covenant. Not every person that you meet is a candidate for covenant either. In fact, there are many people you will meet who will seek to steal from you by making covenant with you. This is why we need to know that our enemy, the devil, is seeking to sow tares into our lives through ungodly people. There will inevitably be someone you meet, an ungodly person, that will seek to enter into covenant with you. They will come into your life and seek to destroy you through their ungodly influence. I want to encourage you, do not make covenant with this type of person, otherwise, you will be responsible for the pain that you experience through them.

Much of the body of Christ today is looking to individuals who have charisma, instead of character. Yet, character is of utmost importance when determining who to make covenant with. The Bible says,

"Most men will proclaim each his own goodness but who can find a faithful man?" (Prov. 20:6)

There are many people who outwardly look good, but they are not faithful men or women and, as a result, they are not covenant people. When you look at the Hebrew word for faithful, this word literally means: A loyal or covenant keeping person. In other words, it is hard to find a man or woman who will be loyal to their covenant promise.

Men and women of character keep covenant. This is why God is looking to build character into us, as believers, so that we can become covenant keepers. God wants us to have the power of personal character to be covenant makers and covenant keepers, not covenant breakers.

My wife, Joni, is a woman of character. One day, while we were in Branson, MO., at the theme park, Silver Dollar City, both my daughter Janelle, and I encouraged Joni to go on a roller coaster ride called, "Thunderation." Needless to say, Joni is not very fond of roller coasters. Finally after much convincing, she gave in and said, "I will do it because I am a covenant woman." While we all know that we don't have to go on a roller coaster ride to prove our covenant commitment, the Lord, through Joni's statement, gave me a revelation concerning what covenant can be like.

At times, being in covenant can feel like a roller coaster ride. Every covenant relationship has it's high and low, top and bottom experiences. This is why we cannot base covenant on what we feel. There may be times when we will feel loved or unloved, appreciated or unappreciated, on top or at the bottom. These times are designed to test our covenant commitment. Covenant can, at times, mean enduring things that we go through without making it to the end of the ride, and enjoying it as much as possible. Our journey into covenant keeping can be an exciting one, and it certainly beats the alternatives. Because of this, I want to ask you, "Won't you take the ride of covenant with us?"

You can be a covenant keeper. It is not too difficult for those who are in love with Jesus. The fact that you are reading this book shows that you inwardly desire to be a covenant keeper. What I am about to share with you in this book, through the Bible and experience, will help you become a covenant keeper. You, through this book, will mature in Christ and begin walking in His fullness: To such a degree that you will be transformed by the power of this revelation of covenant keeping. Your life will be reformed and conformed to the image of Christ through the mighty impartation of this dynamic revelation into your life. To God be the glory!

Chapter One

Unlocking the Mystery of Covenant

The Word of God has been given to us by God to expand our understanding of Him, and the world around us. We should think big thoughts, for God thinks big thoughts and He wants us to do the same. God has given us His Word, so that He, by His Word, could give us the ability to think His thoughts. God's thoughts are higher than our thoughts, and His ways are higher than our ways; this is why we need to read His Word: to understand the way God thinks. When we read the Word of God, we are looking into the mind of God, for God is the author of the Bible. The Bible is a book given by God to help us understand the ways and thoughts of God.

Within the Word of God, there are mysteries that have been hidden for ages and generations. God has hidden these mysteries within His Word to keep them from being misused by those who superficially study His Word. God has placed within the pages of the Bible the mysteries of the kingdom of God. These hidden mysteries are awaiting discovery by serious students of the Word of God. When we look into the Word of God, we are to be searching for these hidden mysteries, which are a revelation of how the kingdom of God works.

It is God's desire to reveal these hidden mysteries to us by giving us His Spirit of revelation. God wants to reveal the mysteries of the kingdom of God to those who are committed to following Him. We, as His disciples, are to be a people of revelation — we are to be a people who know the mysteries that are hidden within the Word of God.

Revelation did not stop with the death of Jesus, or the Apostles. No! That was just the beginning of the outpouring of the Spirit of revelation into the earth. We, as believers, need to realize that God is still revealing things today. There is still a resounding voice from heaven that is speaking into the earth the secret things of God.

The Holy Spirit has been sent by God to show us what He has given to us, even those things that are yet to come. The Holy Spirit longs to communicate with us about the deep things of Christ's kingdom. Are we being sensitive to the Holy Spirit? Are we waiting for Him to reveal things to us? Are we studying the Word of God to show ourselves approved in the sight of the Savior?

Our Christian lives should be daily filled with a sense of adventure. We should never be bored, for there is so much yet to be discovered. There are so many mysteries hidden within the Word of God just waiting to be unlocked by us, and I believe that one of the greatest of these mysteries is **the mystery of covenant.**

The Revelation of Covenant

It has taken me most of my life to understand this one word — *covenant.* And even now, after years of walking in it, I still feel like a little child at Christmas time waiting to open just one more present: ever yearning to understand the fullness of this mystery called covenant. I have a genuine desire to learn as much as I can about how to keep covenant.

I cannot even begin to tell you how much has happened in my life by understanding the principle of covenant keeping. The blessings I have experienced, through understanding this mystery of covenant keeping, are too immense and unexplainable for me to convey to you. Being in covenant, and among covenant people, has truly caused my life to be blessed beyond belief. This revelation of covenant keeping has blessed my life, and I believe that it will bless yours as well.

Over the years, I have learned many things about covenant. I will share these things with you in this book. You will learn not only what I have learned about covenant, but how I came to understand covenant. I want to show you the process that I went through to get to the place I am today in my walk with God.

I am a covenant man. I am a covenant keeper. I have learned how to walk in and keep covenant with God and godly covenant with others. I know how to make covenant, when and when not to make covenant, and how to truly discern whether a covenant is godly. This is the cornerstone upon which all of my relationships are built: from my relationship with God, to my relationship with my wife, children, church and colleagues.

I live by this revelation of covenant, daily. What I am sharing with you is not the impractical persuasions of someone who has never experienced the power of covenant. No! I know the power available to believers through covenant, and this is why God has called me to write this book.

This revelation of covenant is something that not everyone is willing to embrace. Being in covenant means that we must be willing to embrace the requirements of keeping covenant. The timid, and those who are afraid of commitment, will have a difficult time keeping covenant, for covenant revolves around the word commitment.

Walking in covenant means that we honor and respect authority. It is impossible to walk in covenant with God, and godly covenants with others, if we are not willing to submit and reverence authority. This is why covenant is not for those who are rebellious. We cannot be in rebellion toward an authority from God and still live in covenant with God.

The faithless and unbelieving will not be able to keep covenant, for they will not believe what is written. If we cannot, or do not, believe what is written, how can we walk in the mystery of covenant, which is based upon what is written?

Walking in covenant means that we, as believers, must become committed, sold out, submitted people. Covenant is for those who are loyal, trustworthy and faithful people. It is for those believers who genuinely fear God, have a holy reverence and awe for the things of God — a people who are afraid to rebel against God and His word. Those who know that it is a fearful thing to fall into the hands of the living God, and as such, have learned to shun evil. We must become a people of faith who know that God only reveals His mystery of covenant to those who fear Him.

The revelation of covenant has been lost by much of the church in this generation — we do not fear God. We do not even know that we are supposed to fear Him. The fear of the Lord has been replaced by the fashions of men. We fashion ourselves according to our modern marketing strategies, instead of allowing the potter, God, to mold us into Christ's image through His fear. We need to hear what the Word of God says very clearly: the fear of the Lord is the beginning of what God does in and through us.

When we fear God, we are preparing for new beginnings, for the fear of the Lord is what allows us to see clearly, through God's vision, who we are and where we are going. This is the lens that adjusts our vision to God's way of seeing things. This is why we cannot even begin to understand covenant without first understanding the fear of the Lord.

The fear of the Lord cleanses our mind from the thoughts of this world so that we can begin to think the thoughts of God. When this happens, we will then, through the fear of God, understand the covenant we have with God, and the godly covenants that we are called to keep with others. This is the reason that we must learn to fear God.

The Price of Breaking Covenant

The Church of the Lord Jesus Christ in this nation has lost her fear of God. We no longer know what the fear of the Lord is and how it applies to us. We mock men of God and think it is okay. We steal from the church our tithes and offerings, and think that God will not notice. We, like the world, have come to treat sin lightly. We use other words to describe sin — an addiction, a genetic disorder or even a disease, but we do not call it sin. Why is this? What has caused us to become so uncomfortable with the word sin? Why don't we use it anymore? Have we forgotten that we are all sinners in need of a savior? Could it be that we fear this word because it tells us the state that we are in; not just those who are in the world, but more importantly, those who are in the church?

Much of the church has become a place of anarchy, a place where everyone does their own thing. We have become our own self-appointed judge and jury, and as a result, have become something hideous in the sight of God — covenant breakers.

Many churches are filled with broken covenants. We break the covenants that we have made with others in the sight of God, and then think nothing of it. There is a deeper problem than divorce running rampant in the church as a whole — it is the valley of broken relationships between believers.

We, as believers, have become hardened to the things of God because of the broken covenants that fill the church.

We have a problem in the church not just with divorce, but division. We have divided in the name of Christ over minor disagreements. We have not been willing to lay down our opinions and offenses for the sake of unity. We have not seen the importance that unity plays in our lives. We have forfeited the greater things of God at the altar of our desire to be right. This is why there is so much division in the church, and divorce.

We have a problem: There is just as much divorce and division in the church as there is in the world. Statistically speaking, the church has little margin over the world in the realm of keeping covenant. The road to church is paved with the broken bones of bad relationships. This is why we think that division, which has been the center point of church discussion for years, is okay. We don't think it is wrong for us to be a divided body. Could this be the reason there is so much division and divorce in the church?

The church is not only divided because of what others have done in the past — it is divided because we, in the present, have not learned how to walk in covenant with God and one another. We, as a whole, have lost sight of our responsibility in the sight of God to keep our covenant with Him and godly covenants with one another. We desperately need to see our role and responsibility as covenant keepers restored within the church, and our churches.

A Covenant Keepers Responsibility

Very few believers in our day know how to keep covenant, and many don't even know how to make covenant. This is why I often ask couples who want to get married to meet with me and discuss their marriage plans. I have all the couples that I marry fill out a questionnaire before I will marry them. I do not want any of the couples that I marry getting divorced. I want them to know ahead of time what they are doing by making this covenant of marriage. They need to know why they are getting married. Is it really love that they are in, or lust? And I, as a pastor, need to help them come to this recognition.

It is my responsibility as an appointed leader of the flock to care for God's people by teaching them the importance of making covenant, and their responsibility before God to keep covenant. I want them to know the blessings of covenant, as well as the devastation that can come through broken covenant. The people that I pastor need to know that covenant, especially the covenant of marriage, is not a trivial thing in the sight of God. As such, they need to think through their commitment to keeping covenant before they make covenant.

I, as a pastor, have a responsibility in the sight of God to care for my flock by not only comforting them, but also challenging and if necessary, correcting them. This is why I cannot even begin to imagine a real pastor marrying a couple before checking them out to see if they are really committed to one another.

As pastors, our methods may be different, but our goal should be the same: To raise up godly covenant keepers within our congregations — men and women who know how to build long-lasting relationships in their lives.

It is for this reason that I make every effort to teach people under my care not just by my words, but by my example. I give them, through my life, an example that they can follow so they can learn from me how to make and keep godly covenants.

This is why my wife and I renewed our vows to each other in front of my congregation. I wanted them to see how it should be done. I wanted them to hear my vows to my wife and her vows to me. As you can imagine, this was a time of great joy and many tears. Joni was so touched by this moment that tears of joy began to flow from her eyes. She was unable to speak for several minutes. She was overwhelmed by her memories of what God had done for us. She was showing me, and our congregation, the love that she has for me and the love that I have for her. I know her and she knows me — we really love each other. We are committed to each other and have truly become one through our covenant of marriage. This is godly covenant.

Not only have I set an example of covenant through my own marriage with Joni, but I have made covenant with my congregation. I want my church, World Overcomers Church, to know that I genuinely care for them. I want visitors to know that they are going to be treated well in this place. I want them to know that there is a church they can come to and receive help from God, as well as prayer from His covenant people. This is why I have made this vow of covenant with my congregation:

- I covenant to be the best pastor, by the grace of God, that money can't buy.

- To love and accept you, unconditionally.

- To never compromise the Word of God in your life.

- To not run when the going gets tough, but to stand with, and for you, through thick and thin.

- To impart a fresh anointing of the Holy Spirit to you.

- To pray fervently for you.

- To teach and preach, "thus saith the Lord."

- To keep my relationship with God pure and holy.

- To be ready in season and out of season.

- To allow God to do whatever he desires to do in our midst.

- To protect you from harm or danger.

- To train you to become victorious, overcoming, disciples of Jesus Christ, from the cradle to the grave, as long as Jesus tarries.

Walking as a Covenant Keeper

I am in covenant with great men and women of God. God has put into my life ministers who have mentored and trained me to live and walk in covenant. I am in covenant with major national and international ministries. I am also in covenant with lesser known ministries — those who are well known by God, and me. God has greatly used these individuals to minister to me. I have even been physically healed by the power of God through my covenant with these ministries. These men and women of God have the right to speak into my life whatever they believe God is speaking to them. And I, over the years, have learned to listen to their advise, even when I don't want to hear what they have to say.

I am a man under authority, a man who is submitted, committed and accountable to those men and women with whom I am in covenant. They are my spiritual overseers. They are the godly watchmen that God has set into my life to help me, even as I help others, both in my natural and spiritual family. I am a man who has learned to live within the covenantal relationships in my life.

This is why I am so concerned with pastors in the body of

Christ; there are many pastors and spiritual leaders who do not really understand the nature of covenant. They themselves have not learned to walk in covenant and, as a result, are unable to teach their people how to live in covenant.

This is one reason so many believers today have a tough time developing long-lasting Biblical relationships in their lives. There is a great void in the lives of many believers who desire to have long-lasting relationships, but they are not being taught how to develop them by their spiritual leaders.

As a result, believers today are looking for leaders who are not afraid to get down into the trenches of life with them and help them out of their problems. They want a solid foundation upon which they can build their lives, and relationships. They want examples, spiritual fathers, who are able to show them what genuine covenantal relationships are like. They are searching for answers to the question: Why it is so difficult to build and maintain godly relationships that are filled with love?

The truth is most believers desire to have good godly relationships — we want to love and be loved. God has placed this desire in our hearts.

This is what most believers are looking for today, but few are finding. Instead, there is a steady stream of broken believers who go from broken relationship to broken relationship, and from church to church. Many churches are filled with walking, wounded people searching for something better somewhere. Isn't there something wrong with this picture?

We need to realize that we have become lost in this area of building godly covenants. We need spiritual fathers who will show us the way back to living by covenant. We need spiritual fathers who will turn us back to God and one another. We need to recover the revelation of covenant — a revelation that has been lost for generations.

Many believers today, when they think of covenant, sincerely believe that covenant always involves blood sacrifice. And although the blood covenant is vital to our ability to keep covenant, covenant involves so much more. Don't get me wrong, I believe in the power of the blood and it's importance to covenant, but this is not all that covenant is about.

It is this misunderstanding about the nature of covenant that shows me how close we are to losing the heritage left to us by our spiritual forefathers. This is why we must regain the understanding of covenant they left us through receiving the fear of God.

The fear of the Lord is the birthplace for all godly covenant. Those who desire to build long-lasting relationships in their lives must start at the place of beginnings — the fear of the Lord.

The Key to Understanding Covenant

The Bible tells us,

"The secret of the Lord is with those who fear Him; and He will show them His covenant." (Ps. 25:14)

"The fear of the Lord is clean, enduring forever." (Ps. 19:9)

This is the key that we need to unlock the mystery of covenant. We can only go as far in understanding the mystery of covenant as our holy reverence for God. If we fear God, then He will reveal the mystery of His covenant to us. We will sit with an unveiled face, beholding the beauties of His covenant; we will see the manifest glory resident in living by covenant; and as a result, the covenant life will become plain to us.

This is the reason why so few understand covenant today — we do not fear God. We have not given God His rightful place in our lives. We have lost touch with His hidden reality of covenant through our ungodly alliance with the world. There is little fear of God in the church; we have not recognized who our Holy and Awesome Father, that sits upon the throne of heaven, is. It is this, more than anything else, that we must regain before we can truly understand the mystery of covenant in the very depths of our heart.

We can always bank on God responding to us, if we have a holy awe and reverence for His presence. This is what we need in our day.

Our God is a covenant God. God does everything with man in and through covenant. God will do nothing for man apart from covenant. From the very foundations of the world, man was made to walk in covenant with God. God, from the very beginning of His creation, walked with man in the cool of the day; He was waiting for an opportunity to spend time with His covenant people, Adam and Eve. This is why when God couldn't find man there was such an ache in His heart, God cried out; *"Adam where are you?" (Gen. 3:9).*

19

This is what happens when any of God's covenant people are seduced away from Him. God cries out for each of us saying, *"Where are you?" (put your name here)*

God is looking for a people who will walk in covenant with Him. This is what God desires and longs for from us. Each and everyday, as God looks across the expanse of the earth, He is looking, watching, waiting for someone through whom He can show Himself strong. Truly, God is waiting on us, when so very often, we think that we are waiting on Him. This is why I want you to understand that God will do nothing apart from covenant.

Everything that God does starts with covenant. Covenant is the place where the yoke breaking, burden lifting, tangible anointing and flow of the Holy Spirit, abides. It is here, in the place of covenant, where we see the power and presence of the risen Christ. The anointing comes into the midst of a covenant people to build the kingdom of God — covenant people are kingdom builders. This is why I can say the kingdom of God is, first and foremost, about building godly covenant relationships.

This is what God has called us, as the body of Christ, to do in the earth, till Christ comes: We are called to build the church by building our relationship with God and godly relationships with one another. As we build our relationship with God, and godly relationships with others, a spiritual change starts to take place in the church and it starts to grow.

Our relationships, as we keep covenant with God and godly covenants with others, releases the anointing of God to, literally, destroy the work of the devil: Who is opposed to covenant.

Satan hates godly covenant. The devil doesn't like it when believers come together through covenant, because he knows that covenant relationships are the single greatest threat to his kingdom.

The kingdom of darkness trembles when believers begin to enter into covenant, for they know that it will destroy their hold upon the lives of people. Anarchy, a tool of the devil, will be driven backwards as believers walk in covenant. Lawlessness will be dispelled through the light of believers walking in covenant. Rebellion and witchcraft will be trampled underfoot as believers in the Lord Jesus Christ learn how to walk in godly covenant.

This is why we must learn what covenant is, and how to walk in it, especially, at this very dark hour in the history of this idolatrous generation and perverted nation.

Godly vs. Ungodly Covenant

Now that I have given you a taste of what covenant can do in your life, I am sure that you are asking yourselves the question: What is covenant?

I have done this for a reason: My hope has been to stir up in you a godly desire to become a person of covenant. I want you to desire to become a covenant person so that you will want to learn, what I have to share, about the secrets of covenant.

I have discovered many things about what covenant is, and how it can bring the blessing of God into your life. However, before I can do this, I believe that I must first share with you what covenant is not. Why am I doing this? Because there are many people who, through their own ignorance and deception, have perverted the meaning of covenant. They have polluted this holy word of covenant through their unholy lives. And, instead of allowing the devil to steal yet another word from our Christian vocabulary, I want to clarify what the word covenant means by showing you what it is not.

Covenant is not sharing wives in a communal home, sipping poison in the name of God or becoming blood brothers by sharing blood. We all know, or should know, that these weird things, done in the name of covenant, are not covenant. However, there are some things that everyday people, like you and me, tend to believe is covenant, when it is not.

Covenant is also not allowing your spouse, parents or others to beat or abuse you. This includes obeying our leaders at any cost, even when they have gone astray. These things are not covenant. Yet, I have noticed that good God-fearing people often can be seduced into believing that they are keeping covenant by doing these things. Allowing others to do these things to us is not keeping covenant — it is foolish and dangerous. In reality, these things are the enemy's attempt to deceive and mislead us away from genuine covenantal relationships. This is a very dangerous place for anyone to be in, especially a believer, for it can destroy your whole spiritual life. This is why it is extremely important for us to know what covenant is and how to keep it.

What is covenant? Covenant is a binding agreement made between two people. This agreement goes way beyond words, and is more than the ability to agree over particular issues.

In fact, covenant people will often disagree over particular issues, but then, for the sake of covenant; choose to agree to disagree. This is why there is strength in keeping covenant — we do not need to agree to keep our agreement.

Covenant is *an* agreement with another person and does not necessarily mean that we will be *in* agreement with that person. This means that we cannot use Amos 3:3, which says, *"Can two walk together, unless they are agreed?"* to break covenant over minor disagreements in our relationships. When Amos penned this passage of scripture, he was talking about breaking covenant with people who had slipped into idolatry not minor disagreements in life.

We, when we make covenant, must realize that we are choosing, by an act of covenant; to make an agreement in the sight of God, with God or one another — this is covenant. Covenant is about making *an* agreement with those individuals that God has placed in your life. This is where true love and godly relationships can be found: Making and keeping covenant with those people to whom you have committed yourself.

Finding Covenant Love

Covenant is the only place where we can give and receive real love. Real love does not fear making covenant, because it does not fear being committed. Our love is only as deep as our commitment, to honor the covenant that we have made with those whom God has placed in our lives. Can you see how important the understanding of covenant is to our relationships?

Understanding covenant is a vital ingredient for us to be able to build our relationships on God's love, for unconditional love can only be found in the place of covenant. It is here, in this place of covenant, where we are truly able to learn how to love each other unconditionally. This happens as we disagree over issues, yet are still able to remain in our agreement. Covenant is the super glue that holds our relationships together in spite of the strong disagreements we may have with each other. This means that we, those who abide in godly covenantal relationships, have someone, with whom, we can share the deepest secrets of our soul.

Covenant is a place of complete trust, it is a place where we

22

know that we share the secrets of our hearts without compromising or destroying our relationships. This is what makes covenant people willing to be submitted and committed to God and each other.

Covenant people are loyal and trustworthy disciples of Christ, they are people who are willing to be held accountable for their actions before both God and man. They are genuine people who have an ability to stand strong in the face of adversity, because they know that there is someone who is willing to stand with them through their times of crisis. Times of crisis knit those who are in covenant together, instead of tearing them apart. God has made heart to heart relationships available to all of us through the vehicle of covenant.

Covenant relationships are the strongest kind of relationships that man can ever know. Why is this? Because genuine covenantal relationships are not based upon the casual convenience offered by the world, but committed care revealed to us by God's unconditional love. As such, covenant people are willing to care for and lift up their covenant partners. This is the burden of responsibility that they gladly bear because of the blessing that covenant people share. Covenant is a two-way street that does not just involve blessing, but also includes responsibility.

Being in godly covenant with others has been designed by God to be a place of blessing. God has pronounced blessing upon those who walk in covenant. Covenant is where we are connected to one another so that we can be protected by one another. This is why the Bible tells us,

"Behold how good and pleasant it is for brethren to dwell together in unity!" (Ps. 133:1)

It is good for us to be in unity; for it is here, according to the Bible, where,

"The Lord commanded the blessing — Life forevermore." (Ps. 133:3)

There is no better way to see the blessing of God come upon your life than covenant. When you choose to keep covenant with God, and godly covenants with others, you open yourself up to the tremendous blessings that God has prepared for you since the foundation of the world. The way of covenant is the way to the blessing of God. You will trip over blessings when you enter into the place of covenant. They will come upon you and overtake you just because you choose to keep covenant with God and godly covenant with others. This is what God has promised for all those who keep covenant and obey His Word.

Keeping covenant and obeying the Word of God are one and the same thing. If we are truly covenant keepers, then we will obey the Word of God and do what God tells us to do. It is impossible to be in covenant with God and not keep His Word.

For example, the Bible tells us,

"If someone says I love God and hates His own brother; he is a liar... And this is the commandment that we have from Him that he who loves God must love his brother also." (1 John 4:20,21)

You cannot hate your brother and still love God, according to the Bible. If we say that we love God, but do not love our brother, we are lying to ourselves, and not really keeping the covenant that God has set before us. This is what the Bible calls, *"deceiving yourself"* (James 1:22).

We can deceive ourselves into believing a lie — we may even believe that we are doing the Word of God: Keeping covenant with God and godly covenants with others, when we really aren't. It is easy to do this; many of us have done it, that is, until we are convicted by the Holy Spirit of our error.

When we come under conviction, we must choose to repent of what we are doing, otherwise, we have consciously chosen to remain in violation of our covenant with God or godly covenants with others. This is what the Bible calls — *covenant breaking* — this is not a good place to be in for it is here where we are vulnerable to the schemes of our adversary: Satan.

If you are a believer who has succumbed to Satan's strategies, you don't have to stay there; you can be delivered from that barren place. The Bible says,

"the truth will make you free." (John 8:32)

This is why God comes to us with His truth: to help us overcome the deception that we are susceptible to as human beings. If you have struggled in this area, you are not alone; we have all had to repent of various things hindering us in our walk with God. I want to encourage you, you can do it, let go of whatever holds you back, and enter in to the blessings of keeping covenant again.

God will forgive you. And He will cause His favor to fall upon your life again. You will be restored to a better place in your walk with Him than before. The favor of God will rest upon you and your life. This is what God wants to do, if you have fallen away from keeping your covenant with Him or godly covenant with others.

Because of this, I want to encourage you to trust God for restoration to take place in your life. Believe Him for it, and He will do it. God wants to impart to you supernatural favor, through the restoration of your covenant with Him and godly covenants with others. Let Him do this in your life by walking in a humble heart of repentance.

Your life is about to change — you are going to receive favor from on high — as you allow God to renew your desire to keep your covenant with Him and godly covenants with others.

Favor: A Covenant Keeper's Reward

One of the main blessings of keeping covenant with God and godly covenant with others is favor with God and man. God gives favor to those who keep their covenant with Him and godly covenants with others.

What is favor, and why is it so important? Favor is the supernatural blessing of God that causes you to have special privileges in the sight of both God and man. Favor gives you the advantage in every area of life. You will have an advantage over those around you — not only in church, but on your job, in your home and with your family. God will literally give you one up on everyone around you. People will wonder, *"why do all those good things happen to you?"* They will say, *"how is it that you are always in the right place, at the right time, doing the right thing all the time?"* And the only thing that you will be able to say is: ***"It's the favor of God."*** It is the favor of God that gives those who keep covenant supernatural privilege, and advantage, in the sight of God and man. This should make you excited! I know it does me.

Since the time I was called into ministry at 4 years old, till today, God has richly blessed me with favor. I have people who marvel at who I know and my intimate circle of friends. They ask me, *"how is it that you have so much favor?"*

I have favor with several major sports figures. My dad was shocked when I told him that we were going to spend quality time with a baseball sports legend. At first, he couldn't believe it. This is the kind of favor God has given me among world famous athletes.

I also have favor with major national and international ministries. I have been invited to major crusades around the nation, at no charge to myself, under the care and covering of these great men of God. I have even been invited on national television to share my testimony of God's healing power. These things normally just don't happen to people, but God has blessed me with supernatural favor.

God will give you favor where you want it. You will receive the supernatural blessing and favor of God in the things that you truly enjoy. God will bless you with what you want, in the things that you want it in, as you walk in covenant with Him.

I personally enjoy sports and ministry, and this is where God has given me favor. I enjoy being able to sit next to Bull's players during a game. I enjoy being around famous baseball athletes. I desire to spend quality time with great men of God. I want the anointing on their life to be deposited into mine. Do you want to know why God has given me favor in these areas? It is not because I am someone special, even though, I like to think of myself as special in God's eyes. It is because I keep covenant with God and godly covenants with others.

The church that I pastor, World Overcomers Church, has become, according to major church leaders, one of the most anointed churches in the nation. God has not only enabled us to grow as a church, but has given us a great building to meet in. We purchased a 1.5 million dollar building, including a sizable expansion of the existing facilities. God, by His favor, gave us this building, even though several other churches wanted it. There were already three churches meeting in this building before we moved in, and they wanted to buy this building, but God gave it to us. This is almost unbelievable, isn't it? Do you want to know what makes things like this happen? I can tell you in one word: *favor.*

God has granted this church favor because we have learned how to keep our covenant with God and godly covenants with others. The church that I pastor is mostly filled with covenant keepers. People who come to World Overcomers Church know how, and have been willing to learn how, to keep covenant with God and godly covenants with others. We have received tremendous blessings from God because we, as a covenant keeping community of believers, are living under the favor of God.

Living Life to the Fullest

Have you yet captured a glimpse of how important this mystery of covenant is to you and me? I am telling you the secret of living life to it's fullest. I am giving you practical instructions on how to walk in the fullness of God's blessing. Yes, God wants to bless you! The Bible tells us that God has things prepared for you that you don't even know about at this time. God is ready and willing to give you what He has prepared for you. God is waiting for you to do something. What is He waiting for? He is waiting for you to become a covenant keeper.

Please! Please, as you read this book, allow it to sink deep into your heart. There are so many things waiting for you, already prepared for you, just waiting for you to take a step toward becoming a covenant keeper. Will you make a commitment to keep covenant with God and godly covenants with others?

I can tell you, from experience, that your life will never be the same again. You will receive the power of personal favor from God, with both God and man. This is one of the greatest blessings that you can ever receive, and it is available to you through the mystery of covenant keeping.

I hope that you can sense the impartation of favor that is being given to you by the Holy Spirit. Right now, even as you are reading this book, God is imparting favor into your life. You are receiving favor from God. The favor on my life is being imparted to you by the Holy Spirit through this message on covenant keeping. You are receiving a mighty impartation of the anointing of favor through this book.

Why is this happening? Because you are learning how to use the key of covenant keeping to release the blessing of God's favor into your life. The door of God's favor is swinging wide open to you, even as you make a quality decision to become a covenant keeper. You are about to experience a period of unparalleled blessing in your life.

The blessing of God's favor is coming upon you now, even as you, in your heart, decide to grow in your knowledge and ability to keep covenant with God and godly covenants with others. This is the key that will unlock the door of supernatural victory in your life. To God be the glory!

God is about to do wonderful things in your life. Why? Because you are starting a journey into the greatest adventure known to man: Living the covenant life. You are learning how to become a covenant keeper, as well as how to avoid breaking covenant. God is calling you up into a higher place, a place called covenant living.

What is covenant living? Covenant living is a life that is in constant communion with the Creator: it is a life that allows you privilege and advantage, through favor; it is a life of blessing and protection; and it is a life of obedience to the voice and word of God. The covenant life is the greatest life available to mankind. Just think about this for a second, you not only have a word from God, but a covenant with Him. You have a word that is irreplaceable and irrevocable before Almighty God, a covenant.

This is why you are special in the sight of God. This is what puts a glow in God's eyes when He sees you — His covenant with you. This is what God sees when He looks at you. You have authority in the sight of God through your covenant with Him. You can, through keeping covenant with God and godly covenant with others, make up the hedge and stand in the gap for those around you. You can stop the schemes of Satan by keeping covenant with God and godly covenants with others.

Are you ready to move forward in understanding covenant? Can you see how important understanding this mystery of covenant is? Are you ready to enter into covenant living: a life of keeping covenant with God and godly covenants with others? I believe that you are, but before we go any further in this book, I think it would be helpful for us to see where we are as covenant keepers today. This is why I have developed several questions to help determine the level and extent of your covenant keeping knowledge and ability. I want you to see where you are right now as a covenant keeper, so you can see how you are growing as a covenant keeper. This test is strictly for self examination and personal meditation.

The Covenant Test

1.   Am I believing the best of others?

2.   Are my relationships with others short-lived?

3.   Am I building up and edifying others?

4.   Do I serve God and others?

5.   Do I submit to authority only when I agree?

6.   Do I easily get offended?

7.   When my relationships are tested, do I run?

8.   Am I able to trust others?

9.   Is my motivation "thy or my kingdom come"?

10.   Am I passionately in love with God?

Chapter Two

Living in Covenant Relationships

How did you do on the self-evaluation questions in the last chapter? If you haven't taken it yet. I would encourage you to go back and take it now. Why should you do this? So that you can grow in your understanding of covenant as you read through the rest of this book.

Contrary to what you may have thought, these questions do have correct answers. I did not just create these questions for the purpose of your own self-evaluation, but to help you see where you need to grow in your understanding of covenant. I want you to see where you may misunderstand covenant right now, so that you can grow in your understanding of covenant as you read through the rest of this book.

Additionally, I want you to see how the change in your understanding of covenant tangibly affects your life and relationships. I want you to become a walking witness of the power resident in covenant living. To God be the Glory!

Before I go any further in this chapter, I believe it is important for you to know this: What is happening in your life, at this moment, is based upon your level of understanding of covenant.

God does nothing without covenant, and what God does do is determined by your covenant with Him. God looks at His covenant with you, before He looks at you. Then when He does look at you, He deals with you on the basis of your covenant.

This is why God tells us to bring Him into remembrance of His covenant promises. Not that God has lost His mind or memory — He has not. No! God desires for us to deal with Him on the basis of our covenant, not our needs. Because of this, God will often point us back to His covenant with us when we are asking Him to meet our needs. When God does this, He is not being unsympathetic to us, but He is seeking to meet us and our needs on the basis of our covenant with Him. Why does God do this? So that we can become His covenant people, and He can establish His covenant in the earth.

Becoming a Covenant Keeper

We are called to be a covenant people. This is the highest calling upon believers, in general, and the body of Christ, specifically. We are to be God's covenant people, living in constant covenant with HIm. This is what God looks and longs for: A people who are devoted to their covenant with Him.

Yet, when God looks across the body of Christ, very often what He sees is far different from what He wants to see. Instead of seeing His church walking in covenant as a whole, He sees a small group of people in the church called, *the remnant*, who have learned how to live by their covenant with Him.

This remnant of believers, as the Bible calls them, has learned how to become covenant keepers. They are a covenant people who have learned how to keep covenant with God and godly covenants with others. They have learned the secret to living in the blessing and favor of God: Living in godly covenantal relationships.

God, by His covenant with this covenant people, has made them dependable, reliable, grace-motivated believers. They are a people who know how to follow their God and, as a result, are given ability and opportunity by God to lead. Through their understanding of the covenant, they have learned how to live in the blessings of Abraham, and the cross. Christ is their all in all, for they realize how much He has paid to bring them into the place of covenant. As a result, they strive to maintain their covenant with God, through His help, and their godly covenants with others by His help.

Yet within the church, there are many who do not understand the mystery of covenant. Many do not even know that this mystery of covenant exists. It is as if their eyes have been blinded — they cannot see or understand covenant, for they do not fear God.

Even among those who claim to fear God, some are not really committed to Him day in and day out. I am talking about blood washed, sanctified believers who give up their place of covenant when times are tough. They do not know how to stay in their covenant through thick and thin. One day they are hot, the next day they are cold. Their lives are lived like roller coaster rides — they are either going up or down.

As a result, there is no consistency to their lives or relationships; they move from relationship to relationship hoping to find what they are seeking — genuine love. Yet, these wishy-washy believers never find the love they are seeking. And even if, by some miraculous intervention, they do find love — they will often misunderstand it. What these believers are really after is not love, but convenience. They want what they want, when they want it, and will work to do anything they can to get it, but will never receive it, for they are always looking in all the wrong places, for the wrong thing.

I am talking about believers, who go to church, that have slipped into a dangerous place — they have become covenant breakers. For this kind of person, their word is not their bond; they are only there when things are going well, and slip away when times get tough. They have lost the key of knowledge regarding covenant, and the blessing and favor of God. This means that they are ever doomed to repeat their mistakes unless someone shows them the error of their way. This is why I want to ask you a difficult question: Are you a covenant breaker or covenant keeper?

What kind of life are you living for Christ? What and where are your fruits? Are you living for the Lord or just seeking Him during times of need? Jesus is not just looking to meet our needs, but to bring us to the place where He can meet all of our needs — covenant keeping. It is when we keep covenant with God that He meets our needs and answers our prayers.

Covenant keeping is the basis for our prayer life. When we keep covenant with God, and godly covenants with others, God answers our prayers. When we break covenant with God, or godly covenants with others, we have shut down the vehicle through which God has chosen to bring His blessing into our lives. What a sobering thought! We can remove ourselves from living under God's blessing by breaking covenant.

This is why the Bible tells us to be careful when you make a vow, literally, a covenant. Making covenant is a serious matter; we should not deal with it lightly. We should always see covenant making as a serious decision and seek God about the covenants that we make. Why? So we can keep ourselves from making ungodly covenants with others, and then keep the godly covenants we make by God's grace.

A good example of making covenant is David. David kept his word (or covenant) even to his own hurt; according to the Bible. He knew that keeping covenant with God and godly covenants with others was more important than any temporary pain that He might experience through keeping covenant. As a result, David was able to say,

"Let the righteous smite me; It shall be a gentle oil, which shall not bruise my head." (Ps. 141:5)

I wish we all had a heart to keep covenant like David, don't you?

Why Bad Things Happen to Good People

I am amazed by the lack of understanding of covenant in the church. The fact is many of us have never been taught about covenant. No wonder we ask ourselves the question: *"why do bad things happen to good people?"*

Bad things can happen to good people, but God did not call us to only be good people. He has called us to be covenant people. Is there really a difference? Yes! Just because you are good does not mean that you are walking in covenant. You can be a good person and still not be in covenant with God or godly covenants with others. Good people go to hell everyday. This is why we need to hear that there is a difference between just being good and being good by being in covenant.

For such a long time, we have been taught how to be good, but many have not been taught how to live in covenant. The word covenant isn't even in our daily vocabulary. Our words reveal what is in our hearts. The truth of the matter is that many are ignorant of covenant because a majority of leaders have not taught on it. This is an area that has, for the most part, been neglected by leaders through ignorance or fear. And this is why so many believers have been duped by the enemy into believing a lie about covenant. Some, through their own misunderstanding of covenant, fear it; others ignore it. This is why I believe that we need sound teaching about covenant.

We need to hear the truth: There are people who will come across our path that we should avoid making covenant with at all costs. God has not called us to be in covenant with everyone. We are only called to be in covenant with those people that He places into our lives.

Not everyone that I meet is ready to make covenant with me. This is why I like to look at someone's character before I make covenant with them. I will only make covenant with those individuals who I know have decent character. Why is this? Because I know that loyal men and women are faithful to keep their covenant with God and godly covenant with others. They do not hop from covenant to covenant hoping to find the answers to their problems. Instead, they realize that staying in covenant with God and godly covenants with others is the key that will unlock the door to victory over their problems.

Please hear this, I want to help you understand what I understand about covenant. I want to show you not just how to keep covenant, but more importantly, how to determine if you should make a covenant with another person. I am doing this to help you avoid making ungodly covenants with individuals that you should avoid at all costs. I do not want you to fall into the trap of the enemy who is ever seeking to devour from us, what God desires to give us, by causing us to become covenant breakers. What I am sharing with you will help you avoid becoming a poor covenant maker so that you will not become a covenant breaker. And it will help you keep covenant with God and godly covenants with others so that you can be blessed by God.

As we saw in the first chapter, God blesses those who keep their covenants. God will, in fact, do nothing apart from covenant. This is why I want you to understand that what is happening in your life right now is dependent upon your present covenant relationships. The degree to which you are making and keeping your covenant with God and godly covenants with others is the degree to which you are being blessed by God.

It is impossible to receive the blessing of God without first becoming a covenant keeper. The covenant life is a blessed life, and this is why I want to help you learn how to live in covenant with God and godly covenants with others. I want to see you blessed. God wants to bless you. He is waiting on you to learn the secret to His blessing — covenant living. The covenant life is a blessed life, a joyful life, a life satisfied by living water that streams from God's very own presence. You can enter into this living stream of life giving covenant. You can become a covenant keeper, no matter what you have done in the past. You can live fully for God and fulfill your destiny, as a believer, through this godly vehicle of blessing — covenant keeping.

Choosing the Fear and Favor of God

You not only have the responsibility to become a covenant keeper, but you have the right as well. God has given you the power to become a covenant keeper. You don't need to wander through life any longer wondering if things will ever change. You already have an answer in the Word of God, a covenant promise. You have been given something far better than silver and gold — you have received a Word from God. God has already told you that He will bless you, if you keep covenant with Him and godly covenants with others.

Please listen, what I am sharing with you will truly help you. It will cause you to receive the manifold blessings of God. You will be so blessed that blessings will run over from your life and spill into the lives of others. I know, I have experienced it. Wouldn't you like to experience this place of continual blessing? You can! How? By going to the place of beginnings: the fear of the Lord.

The fear of the Lord is the beginning of God's work in our lives; it is where we learn how to keep covenant. The fear of the Lord preserves and protects us from making ungodly covenants. It removes us from those who would harm us by breaking covenant with us. The fear of the Lord puts us in a place of vision where we can clearly see the motives of others. It places us above the crowd so that we can view things through God's eyes. The fear of the Lord gives us a clear vision of where we are at and where we should be going. It is what causes us to stay on track so that we can keep our covenant with God and godly covenants with others.

This is why the psalmist said,

"Come, you children, listen to me; I will teach you the fear of the Lord." (Ps. 34:11)

The psalmist knew that the fear of the Lord would keep his own children, and God's children, on track in their walk with God and others. This is the reason he wanted them to hear what he had to say about the fear of the Lord.

Jesus delighted in the fear of the Lord. It was His fear of God that caused Him to stay in tune with His Father, even on His way to the cross. What a powerful example that Jesus has left us! Jesus has shown us, by His example, what the fear of the Lord can do in our lives. And if Jesus needed, even delighted, in the fear of God, shouldn't we be willing to do the same?

Making Godly Covenant

I hope that you are being challenged by what I am writing. This book is designed to keep you from being destroyed through the devices of the devil. I am trying to show you how to avoid making ungodly covenants with others. In 2 Timothy 3:1-5, it says,

"But know this also that in the last days perilous times will come. For men will be lovers of themselves, lovers of money, boasters, proud, blasphemers, disobedient to parents, unthankful, unholy, unloving, unforgiving, slanderers, without self control, brutal, despisers of good, traitors, head-strong, haughty, lovers of pleasure rather than lovers of God having a form of godliness but denying its power. And from such people turn away!"

What a description for the times now facing us. (Because I believe what Paul said in this passage of scripture is so important, I have dedicated Chapter 3 to explaining it fully). We are living in perilous times. We are living in a second dark ages. Men have given themselves over to the devil to commit wickedness. This is why Paul says,

"Now the Spirit expressly says, that in the latter times, some will depart from the faith, giving heed to deceiving spirits and doctrines of demons." (1 Tim. 4:1)

We are in the fight of our lives, and in this war there are winners and losers. The only difference between those who win and lose is who we listen to and follow. Are we listening to God or the devil? Are we walking in the wisdom of God? Or have we chosen the wisdom that is earthly, sensual, even devilish? These questions are vital to our ability to enter into good godly covenants, and they will preserve us from making ungodly covenants.

When we make covenant, it should never be on the basis of earthly wisdom. What is earthly wisdom? It is the wisdom of men based upon what we can see (*i.e. we remain in covenant with the pastor only as long as he smiles at us*). We should never make covenant based upon what we see in the natural through our five senses. We should never make covenant upon what we know according to the flesh. This is why we should never enter into marriage based upon what we see in the natural.

I have seen so many people who married the wrong person because they made their marriage covenant based upon lust, rather than love. They were pleased with the other persons flesh and, as a result, were deceived by it into making an ungodly covenant. They married this person not on the basis of love, but lust, and, through this, they gave place to the devil. When we make covenant this way, we literally throw the door open to the devil and invite him to come in to our lives, for we are using his wisdom.

The devil's wisdom is fleshly and sensual — he feeds on it. The devil will eat our lunch, so to speak, if we make covenant in this way. This worldly wisdom will cause us to be seduced by the devil. We will eventually deny the one who bought us, if we lean upon the arm of the flesh, and be thrown into the realm of the demonic. This is why I want to encourage you to never make covenants on the basis of what you can see physically, for it will always lead you in the wrong direction: Away from God and godly covenants.

What is a godly covenant? A godly covenant is an agreement established between two people who have been joined together by the Spirit of God. It is an agreement made in spirit that is deeper than what can be seen by the two parties entering that agreement. This agreement is based upon something greater than their own individual desire for fellowship — they have been brought and joined together by God for a purpose.

This is why the love covenant people feel for each other is

stronger than the natural love they can normally feel for another person. Covenant love is so strong that it can abide even beyond death, for it is a love stronger than death. The love that I am talking about is the agape love of God. It is an unconditional love that has been put in our hearts by the Holy Spirit. God Himself, has joined us together, such that, it is extremely difficult to break this bond of covenant. I believe that one of the best examples of this type of godly covenant is the covenant that was made between Jonathan and David.

A Godly Example of Covenant

When we look at Jonathan and David, we learn what godly covenant is all about. Jonathan and David were brought together by the hand of God. God joined them together so that they might be protected by each other. David was called to protect and bless Jonathan, and Jonathan was called to bless and protect David. God joined them together in covenant relationship to bring to pass His will in their lives and the nation of Israel. Jonathan and David were put together by God so that God, through them, could bring Israel into the place that He wanted it: Under the rule of a godly king, namely, David.

Jonathan recognized that David was called to be king, even though he was in line to succeed Saul. Jonathan refused to look at things according to the natural. Instead, he chose to believe what he saw by the Spirit: The anointing of God upon David and the God of the anointing upon David. As a result, David and Jonathan became true covenant brothers — brothers joined through genuine covenant — such that their very souls were knit together.

Jonathan loved David as himself. This is why when Saul, his father, started throwing spears at David, he feared for David's life. Jonathan was willing to put himself at risk to protect David: A man whom he loved as his own soul. David knew that he could rely upon Jonathan his covenant brother. David knew that no matter who stood against him Jonathan would stand with him. David and Jonathan had a friendship that was not based upon what they saw in the natural, their relationship was supernatural: They were joined together by the very hand of God.

God joined David and Jonathan together to accomplish His purposes in Israel. God gave to David an ally that could protect him from the hand of Saul. Jonathan became the man David leaned upon to learn what Saul was planning against him, and as a result, was able to avoid deadly conflicts with Saul. David used the wisdom of God, and listened to the council of his friend, Jonathan, so that he could avoid being killed by Saul. God protected David through his covenant relationship with Jonathan, and opened the way for him to be made king in Saul's place.

Have you yet begun to glimpse the importance of godly covenants? Do you see how important it was for David and Jonathan to be in a covenant relationship? David's life depended on his covenant relationship with Jonathan. This brings up some very interesting questions: Would Saul have been able to kill David, if Jonathan had not stood by him? What if David had avoided making covenant with Jonathan because he was Saul's son — would he have survived? The point that I am trying to make with these questions is this: I believe there are many David's today who are not in covenant with their Jonathan, and there are many Jonathan's today who are not in covenant with their David.

Why is this true? What is keeping believers from entering into godly covenant? I believe that one of the main reasons is that we are too busy living our fast paced lives. Many believers are not willing to take the time necessary to develop intimate covenant relationships. Could this be one of the main reasons why we place such little importance upon covenant in the modern church?

I believe, for the most part, we do not understand the power of genuine covenant relationships. As a result, we often succumb to the strategies of Satan who offers us his counterfeit version of covenant — casual non-committal relationships.

We want to be in covenant, but on our own terms and in our own way. We do not, by and large, want covenant according to the Word of God.

I believe that I am hitting a root that has given birth to rotten fruit in the body of Christ, especially among the churches in America.

Building Covenant Relationships

The church as a whole in the nation of America does not want to develop strong relationships. Instead, we are satisfied by the status quo Christianity cultivated week in and week out in churches around the nation. Poor evangelism isn't the problem with the lack of church growth in America — it is our fervency. We, for the most part, are not willing to pay the price necessary to share our faith. The truth is we are more comfortable sitting in our pews, than sharing our lives.

There is an air of superficiality in the church. We are not willing to be open, honest, transparent people who are in covenant with God and each other. This is why we fear confessing our faults to one another: We do not want to be seen for who we really are — Genuine people who have come to love Jesus. Instead, most of the church prefers to present a false image of reality, a reality that is shaped by the masks that we wear at church on Sunday.

We have lost the understanding that we are the church. We are God's covenant people. We are called to be in covenant with one another. This is what true fellowship is all about. The church is, in fact, the only place where we can find true fellowship. We, the body of Christ, are called to be in covenant relationships with other members of the body. This is the place of protection that God has given us from the schemes of our enemy, Satan.

What about your covenant relationships with others? Do you see how important they are to you? Have you begun to understand the importance of covenant in your life? Walking in covenant is a life or death issue. We are able to live life to it's fullest only when we walk in godly covenants. When we walk outside of godly covenants, we will reap the wages of our choice — death.

With connection, through covenant, comes the blessing of protection from that covenant. Your protection, from the schemes of Satan, is dependent upon who you are in covenant with as a believer. This is why the Bible warns us,

"Do not be unequally yoked with unbelievers." (2 Cor. 6:14)

When we yoke ourselves with the world, we will eventually be trapped by it, and as a result, we will be overcome by the enemy of our soul. God doesn't want this to happen to us. This is why we need to avoid making covenant with those who are worldly: Those who live according to the ways of the world, even among believers.

As believers, we need to test the character of those we make covenant with before we make covenant with them. We need to intimately know the people that we are joining before we connect ourselves to them through covenant. We do not want to be hurt by friendly fire, do we? No! We want faithful men and women, who are covenant keepers, standing alongside us no matter what may come. We want those who are willing to be linked with us hand in hand, arm in arm, shield to shield and faith to faith.

This is the power and protection offered to us through the blessing of genuine covenant.

Covenant vs. Control

Why then, do so many people fear entering into covenant? I believe that the main reason for this is we, for the most part, have not genuinely understood the nature of covenant. Many have confused covenant with control. This is why we need to know that covenant should liberate us, not bring us into bondage. Covenant is designed by God to help us grow in every area of life.

Control, on the other hand, hinders us from growing — it prevents us from becoming who we were made to be, and robs us of our God-given individuality. God did not make us to live under the oppression. No, covenant does not mean unconditional submission to authority. We should never submit to abuse, especially from leaders.

Paul when writing to the believers in Corinth made it clear, in no uncertain terms, that what they are putting up with, by men who claim to be apostles, was not of God. Paul basically tells them they are in covenant with the wrong crowd: Men who are false apostles. Paul, candidly, tells the Corinthian believers that they don't need to put up with those who are bringing them into bondage; those who are taking from them; those who are devouring them; those who are exalting themselves; and those who are striking them on the face (2 Cor. 11:20). What a perfect picture Paul paints for us regarding the attitudes surrounding ungodly covenant! We need to avoid falling into this trap of the enemy.

Ungodly covenants can be summed up in one word — control. This is how ungodly men and women seek to influence us. Paul was warning of people who would come across our path and entrap us through ungodly covenant or control. Ungodly covenants are one of the primary ways that the enemy seeks to bring us into bondage. Ungodly covenants are built upon control — this is what gives them their strength. Whenever we allow someone to exercise control over us, *(and please do not confuse control with godly submission),* then we are giving place to the enemy through an ungodly covenant.

This is why we must avoid control, otherwise, it will destroy the good covenant relationships that we have. We must be on guard against control, for this is one of the main ways that the enemy seeks to sneak into our godly covenant relationships. We must close the door to the devil and ungodly covenants by developing an attitude toward covenant that is found in the book of 2 Corinthians 8:5 which says,

"they first gave themselves to the Lord and to us by the will of God." (2 Cor. 8:5)

Notice they gave their hearts: first to the Lord, then to Paul and those ministering with him. This is what real covenant is all about, It is about us being willing to give our hearts, first to the Lord, then to those He joins us with through covenant.

I hope that you can see what I am trying to convey about the benefits of godly covenant. I am showing you our willingness to be involved in godly covenants enables us to build up the hedge and stand in the gap for one another. This is what covenant is all about.

Covenant is a heartfelt commitment that causes us to join ourselves to another person, a covenant partner. Covenant is a commitment made between two people to join their lives together for a common goal. This means that I cannot only be in covenant with you, but you also must be in covenant with me, otherwise, the bond of covenant is broken. The place of covenant is a place of relationship; it is a place of deep commitment, not casual choice. Covenant is a bond of love that has joined two people together in unbroken harmony so they both can fulfill the purposes of God for their lives.

This is what the marriage covenant is supposed to be. Marriage should be two people joined together in unbroken harmony helping each other fulfill the will of God for their lives.

Our families are meant to be a place where everyone is allowed to be themselves and grow in who God made them to be.

The church is called to be a place where people are not frustrated, regulated and intimidated by each other, but loosed into their position and calling in Christ. All of us, no matter how big or small we think we are, are necessary parts of the body of Christ. None of us is greater than all of us. This is genuine covenant.

The Gift of Godly Covenant

Covenant is not something that we should fear, rather it is something we should cherish as a gift from God for this is what it is. God has given us the privilege of being in covenant with other people. In fact, from the moment we are born, we are born into covenant. This is powerful!

Every child, whether that of a believer or unbeliever, should be in covenant with their parents. This is why God gave us the commandment,

> *"Honor your father and mother, which is the first command with promise: that it may be well with you and you may live long on the earth." (Eph. 6:2,3)*

This is the first command, according to Paul, that God gives each of us along with a promise — that we will have a good and long life on earth. Paul is telling us that keeping covenant is a blessing not only to our parents, but also to us. Paul is showing us the oldest commandment with a promise, because it invites us to cherish the covenant partners that God places into our lives.

We did not get to choose our parents, but we do get to choose our covenant friendships. These relationships also hold a promise for us from God if they are truly from Him. It is as if Paul is inviting us to choose our covenant relationships wisely, for he knows that they will have a deep impact upon our lives.

This is what I am encouraging you to do. I want you to understand that covenant is designed by God to be a blessing if we choose our covenant relationships wisely. We need to know who we are making covenant with before we join ourselves to them, and even then, we need to make sure it is an act of the Holy Spirit, not a work of the flesh. We need to ask ourselves the question: Why am I seeking to make covenant with this person? We need to look beyond the surface and see what we are doing from God's perspective.

The only way we can do this is by laying down our vision of who we are and pick up the vision of God for our lives. We need to find out who God has called us to be and what He has called us to do. This is a good foundation upon which to build our covenants, for covenant is built upon faith not feelings.

Living in covenant requires us to live beyond what we can see. It calls for us to walk by faith and not by sight, looking into the realm of the Spirit, so that we can see what God sees and hear what He hears. The covenant life is a life of faith founded upon the principles of God's Word and ordered by the Holy Spirit. It is a life of relationships that are ordained by God.

Living in covenant is for spiritual people, not spooky people. Flaky people avoid covenant because they want things their own way. They think they are following Christ, but, in reality, are having vain visions that produce nothing. In the end, their lives are filled with turmoil because they want to live in the blessing of God, but not walk in covenant with God or godly covenants with others. This is what separates the fruits and flakes from the followers of Christ, those who are genuinely being led by the Spirit.

The Holy Spirit may call for us to do something unconventional, or out of the ordinary, but He will never cause us to lose our minds in the process. We are to be rooted and grounded in love, covenant love, built upon covenant relationships. This is the call upon every believer in the body of Christ.

Every believer is called to live in covenant. In fact, the rest of this chapter is devoted to talking about the six main areas of covenant that we are called to walk in as believers.

The Six Main Areas of Godly Covenant

There are six main areas of covenant which believers have been called to walk in by God.

I learned about these six areas of covenant through personal experience and study of the Bible. I live in these six areas of covenant, everyday, It is here where I have learned about the covenant life, and covenant relationships.

I have become a person who longs to live in the realm of covenant. As such, I have had to put into practice what I am sharing with you. Walking in covenant is not for the faint of heart. There are many times when it would have been easier for me to lay down my covenants in these six areas, and walk away.

Yet instead of walking away from my covenants during these times, I chose to remain faithful to them.

This is why I want to encourage you to remain faithful to God and others in these six main areas of covenant that I am about to share with you. You will be blessed as you do this.

If there are six main areas of covenant that we are called to walk in as covenant keepers, what are they?

The Six Main Areas of Covenant

1. Our Covenant with God
2. The Marriage Covenant
3. The Parental Covenant
4. The Brotherly Covenant
5. The Believer's Covenant
6. Covenant with Our Leaders

We are all called to live our lives according to these six main areas of covenant. These covenants are the boundaries that God has set for every man, woman and child on earth. No one can break these godly covenants without experiencing a deep sense of personal loss. These are the ties that bind and bring meaning to our lives.

In today's day and age, many people like to think of themselves as independent individuals who are not dependent upon anyone. Yet the Truth is we are very dependent upon God and those that He has placed in our lives. These six areas of covenant are the cords binding our lives to others. These are the people we often flee from, for they constrain us to live a certain way. Yet these boundaries and constraints, are not only restraints to us, but to the enemy.

It is our covenant with God and godly covenants with others that provide us with a haven of protection. This is where we can run and hide when we come under attack from the enemy. We can usually count on these people to back us no matter what. Why? Because God, not man, has put them into our lives for this very purpose. The Bible says,

"A brother is born for adversity... But there is a friend who sticks closer than a brother." (Prov. 17:17, 18:24)

When we go through tough times, we need God, our family

and those true friends that God has placed into our lives. We need these people to support and help us through these difficult times. They are the ones to whom we can and should turn to for help. God has placed them into our lives for these times when our world seems to be falling apart.

This is why when any one of these six areas of covenant are out of balance our lives can be thrown into degrees of chaos. The closer the relationship, and the greater the covenant; the more difficult the experience and challenge of broken covenants to our lives.

Among these six covenants our covenant with God is the one vital to our spiritual survival. From the beginning of creation, we were made to be in covenant with God. As such, this is the closest and most important covenant that we can ever experience.

Our Covenant with God

Our covenant with God is the primary covenant of mankind. Without this covenant; we are living in a spiritual black hole called spiritual death. Without this covenant; we are lost souls doomed to die a grievous death resulting in everlasting sorrow and shame. This is why I want to ask you: are you in covenant with God? The Bible tells us,

"all have sinned, and fallen short of the glory of God."
(Rom. 3:23)

This is why we desperately need to be in covenant with God. We are all sinful people, born in a sinful world, separated from God through the fall of Adam and Eve. The only access we have to God, and the only way to heaven, is through covenant. This is why we need to make covenant with God.

God has given us a great privilege: to be in covenant with Him. He is no respecter of persons in this area. Everyone is welcome! No one who truly desires to be in covenant with God will ever be refused. We can bank on this, it is a personal promise to us from God. If this is true, how then, can we make covenant with God?

God has made it is easy for us. Do you remember what covenant is? Covenant is a binding agreement made between two or more people. God's Word says,

"if you confess with your mouth the Lord Jesus and believe in your heart that God has raised Him from the dead, you will be saved." (Rom. 10:9)

"whoever will call on the name of the Lord Jesus will be saved." (Rom. 10:13)

This is how you can make covenant with God today. Do you want to be in covenant with Him and enter into the blessings of that covenant? Then believe, call upon and receive Jesus as your Savior and Lord. Only believe! When you do this, you will be gloriously saved through a new covenant with God our Heavenly Father, and enter into the great family of God.

The Marriage Covenant

The second main area of covenant is the covenant of marriage.

Marriage is a foundational covenant to our lives; for it is the foundation of the family. Without this godly covenant, there is no sense of legitimate family, and the family ties that bind are broken.

This is why the Bible places sex in the marriage bed. Without the godly covenant of marriage to hold sexual partners together, they will inevitably separate. When this happens, it will destroy any sense of family for children conceived through sexual relations. These children, according to the Bible, are illegitimate children — they are children born outside of the covenant of marriage.

Marriage is the glue that holds life together for our children. Divorce is devastating, especially for our children. Children are the real victims of broken marriage covenants. This is why choosing a spouse and staying within the sexual boundaries of marriage is so important — they are life long commitments.

When we don't abide by these standards, we are abusing the privileges and people that God has placed in our lives. Everyone suffers when a marriage covenant is broken not just the people who break it.

Even society itself suffers, when enough marriage covenants are broken.

The covenant of marriage is a protective covenant provided by God to defend our children, family and even society. Without this godly covenant of marriage, the very fabric of life becomes fragile and starts to unravel at the seams. This is why the marriage covenant is so important — it protects not only us, but our children, family, friends and community.

The Parental Covenant

The third main area of covenant is our covenant as parents.

Parents are responsible for their children, and children are responsible for their parents. Parents are called to bless their children, and children are called to honor their parents. This is the parental covenant.

God gave us the parental covenant as a blessing, for the Bible says,

"children are a heritage from the Lord." (Ps. 127:3)

God, Himself, has blessed us with our children, and we are our parents blessing. This is why the Bible tells us to,

"Honor your father and mother, this is the first commandment with promise: that it may be well with you, and that you may live long on the earth." (Eph. 6:2,3)

I can still remember how, as a child, God called me to care for my mom who was sick with Multiple Sclerosis. I had to do everything for her, because she was bedridden. I did many things that any man, young or old, would never normally do. Why did I do this? Because I knew my responsibility as my mother's son before God.

I knew that God would bless me for caring for my mom. This, plus my desire to keep my covenant with my mom enabled me to sacrifice my time and desires to care for her. God gave me to my mom to be a blessing to her, and I was.

This is why I believe that my children will be a blessing to me. My children will bless me, because I have blessed my parents.

Even now, after years of being married and having my own children, I still know my responsibility as a son. I am still my parents blessing, and as a result, stand to inherit a blessing through them. This is the heritage that I want to pass on to my children — a heritage of blessing.

I want to be blessed by keeping covenant with my parents so that my children can receive this blessing, and pass on the legacy of a godly parental covenant to their children. This is the call of God upon every parent and child.

The Brotherly Covenant

The fourth area of covenant is the brotherly covenant we are called to be in covenant with our natural brothers and sisters. The Bible says,

"a brother is born for adversity." (Prov. 17:17)

God gave us our brothers and sisters to sustain us during hard times. When it seems like there is no one else that we can turn to for help, according to the Bible, we should be able to turn to our brothers and sisters for help — they were born for times like these in our lives.

The Bible teaches us that we are not just gifts to our parents, but we are also gifts to our natural brothers and sisters. God gave us to them for their time of need — this is what family is all about.

The enemy, from the very beginning, has sought to destroy the brotherly covenant.

Cain murdered Abel because of jealousy and greed, and as a result, his entire lineage was cursed. Is this the kind of heritage that we want to pass on to our children? If not, then we need to be careful that we keep godly covenant with our natural brothers and sisters.

God is looking at what we say and do toward our natural brothers and sisters. He is watching to see whether we will keep our godly covenant with them. When we break godly covenant with our natural brothers and sisters, we put ourselves in a dangerous place — a place of separation from the protection brought through our brotherly and sisterly connection.

God has established godly, brotherly, or sisterly, covenants in our lives, for our good, to bring blessing our way. Don't miss out on the blessing that comes from God through your brothers and sisters. Love and help them, and then when you need them, they will be there for you. This is what the brotherly covenant is all about.

The Believer's Covenant

The fifth main area of covenant is the covenant between believers.

Believers, through the blood of Jesus, are in covenant with one another. As we have a responsibility to our natural brothers and sisters, we also have a responsibility to our spiritual brothers and sisters. God has put certain believers in our lives to sustain us through hard times. When things are tough, we know we can turn to them, and they will be there for us. This is what the body of Christ is all about — a spiritual brother or sister is truly born for adversity.

We were not only born-again to be a gift to the Father from the Son; we were born again to be a gift to the church. This is what the church is all about. We, the church, are called to be there for our brothers and sisters. We are commanded in scripture to,

"not forsake the assembling together of ourselves together, as is the manner some." *(Heb. 10:25)*

Those who forsake their local assembly are neglecting their covenant with the church, and as a result, they are breaking covenant with their spiritual brothers and sisters in Christ.

When we backbite, debate and argue with one another over who is right, seeking to get our own way, we are breaking covenant with our spiritual brothers and sisters in Christ.

The body of Christ has been torn through vicious words of gossip, strife, debate and division. This is why Paul spoke so strongly against hanging around with those who cause division. He goes so far as to say, avoid these believers at all costs. This is a strong statement. We would do well to our souls if we kept it — not through fear of the pastor, but rather, fear of the Master.

The body of Christ is about learning how to become submitted, committed, loyal members of the house and family of God not just with our tithes, but also, our lives.

This is the call upon every believer, in every church, among both leader and laity alike.

Covenant with Our Leaders

The sixth main area of covenant is our covenant with our leaders.

If we are genuinely joined by covenant to the church, then, we are also joined by covenant with the leaders of the church. God places the leaders in our lives that He wants us to have. Nothing happens in our lives apart from the hand of divine providence. This does not mean everything happening in our lives is God's will, but it does mean God knows how to get us into His will. God knows what is happening in our lives and He can place the right people in our lives to help us. We can be submitted to the leaders that God has placed in our lives, for we know that God has put them into their position of authority.

How then, can we be submitted and committed to leaders? By first submitting and committing ourselves to God, for He is the one who has put leaders into our lives. This means that we cannot be submitted or committed to our leaders till we are first submitted and committed to God. And this also means when we are not submitted and committed to our leaders, we are not really submitted and committed to God.

Leaders do not have lordship over us, but rather, they have been called by God alongside us to be helpers of our faith. We need them for the impartation that they bring into our lives — not just the gifts, ministries and callings, but of love, loyalty and leadership. Genuine leaders bring into our lives what they possess — the character of Christ.

Christ Himself has set leaders into His church for this purpose: to equip and reveal to us, through their lives, Christ's character. It is Jesus' desire for us to learn from leaders who are walking in His character so that we can begin walking in the same character. And, part of walking in Christ's character is thoughtfully, prayerfully and financially supporting the leaders God has placed in our lives.

Let me ask you a question: When was the last time that you thanked your leaders? When was the last time you prayed for your leaders? When was the last time you put the needs of your leaders, before your own needs? Could it be one of the reasons we are losing leaders within the church is that we are not appreciating the ones that we have?

How many leaders have failed in ministry — not because they sinned or were disobedient to the vision God gave them, but because God's people wouldn't support God's vision? It is tough for me to imagine anything more disappointing than a genuine vision from God failing because God's people broke covenant with their leaders. I can only imagine how the heart of God breaks over this situation.

I hope that you can hear what I am saying, for it is vital that we understand our role in supporting leaders. When we do not support our leaders, we are actually breaking covenant with them. The Bible commands us to,

"not muzzle an ox while it treads out the grain." (1 Tim. 5:18)

Paul, when he wrote this, said, in very clear terms, this was written for the sake of ministers who labor in the gospel. Paul was telling God's people to support their leaders. Leaders, according to Paul, should not feel guilty about raising support from God's people. God has called His people to support their leaders through not only their tithes, but also their lives. May God forgive us for the times that we have muzzled leaders by not supporting them. From this point forward, may it never be said of us that we have broken covenant with our leaders by not supporting them — whether that be in our prayers for them or our finances to them.

Trouble Free Living

These are the six main areas of covenant that I have found, and sought to keep in my own life. I have done my best to keep covenant with God and godly covenants with others. As a result, God has blessed me.

God wants to bless you. You are being invited by God to walk in the blessings of godly covenantal relationships. God has already prepared these relationships for you. Your Heavenly Father, spouse, family, friends and leaders are just looking for you to keep covenant with them this is what they want. Deep down, isn't this what you really want?

Why then do we so often, ignorantly or willfully, stumble into breaking our godly covenants with others? Sometimes it is because we lose sight of the fact that we are in covenant with them, or we may even, lose sight of the importance of this covenant relationship to our lives. Often, we can have a *"grass is greener, on the other side, mentality"* when it comes to keeping covenant with God and godly covenants with others.

Keeping covenant can be hard, especially when we don't agree. Yet, it is the godly covenants in our lives, when we make a quality decision to keep them, that keep us from a multitude of troubles. In fact, I believe that one of the main reasons we stumble into trouble is because we break our godly covenants with others.

When we break godly covenants, whether we realize it or not, we are tearing down the walls of protection that God has built around our lives to protect us from the enemy. We need these godly covenants and God-ordained people in our lives for our protection. Without them, it is very easy for us to enter into a dangerous position — being alone with no one to call for help.

Take yourself out of harm's way today by making a quality decision to keep your godly covenants with others. Become a covenant keeper so that you can reap the harvest of blessings that God has prepared for you. You are just a step away from a place of continual blessing — covenant keeping. And, you are just a step away from building relationships that last through keeping your covenant with God and godly covenants with others.

Chapter Three

Keeping Your
First Love First

"But know this, that in the last days perilous times will come: For men will be lovers of themselves, lovers of money, boasters, proud, blasphemers, disobedient to parents, unthankful, unholy, unloving, unforgiving, slanderers, without self-control, brutal, despisers of good, traitors, headstrong, haughty, lovers of pleasure rather than lovers of God, having a form of godliness but denying its power. And from such people turn away!" (2 Tim. 3:1-5)

Wow! What a description for the days in which we live. Paul knew what he was talking about, when he wrote these words of scripture, regarding the last days. This is why I believe that we need to carefully consider what Paul prophesied. We need to know what he said and how to apply it to our lives today. In order for us to do this, we need to know the background behind what Paul wrote to his young son in the faith, Timothy.

Paul penned this letter while in prison. These were his last words on earth, so they must have been extremely important. Paul chose to spend his last days on earth writing to his spiritual son, Timothy. Paul was deeply concerned about what would happen to his spiritual son, Timothy, when he was gone, for he knew his death was near. As a result, Paul wanted to make sure that Timothy knew what would happen in the future so that he could prepare for it. This is why Paul wrote to Timothy about the perilous times that would come in the last days.

Paul did not want Timothy to be caught off guard by the things that would happen in the world. Paul was equipping him, through his letter, to stand up under any pressure — no matter how great that pressure might become. Timothy would now have to be strong, for Paul's departure was at hand.

Paul knew his death was near, and that it would send shock waves throughout the church. Because of this, he was telling Timothy, a now mature man of God, don't be caught off guard by what will happen to you in the coming days. He was painting a picture for his spiritual son as to what the last days would be like. Paul wanted his spiritual son, Timothy, to be thoroughly prepared for the last days, for they would be dangerous times.

Paul was telling Timothy that the coming days, the last days, would be difficult times. Timothy needed to know how to prepare himself, for the last days were starting. Timothy was now in the last days and as such would need to know how to live during these dark times. If what Paul was telling Timothy was true then, how much more are these words for us today? For as I often say, we are truly living in the last of the last days.

I can only imagine what Timothy must have thought as he read Paul's letter — he must have been shocked by it. Paul, his spiritual father, was telling him to get ready for what was coming in the last days. This must have meant Timothy wasn't prepared for it. Paul, his spiritual father, would never have told him this unless he needed to hear it. Paul's letter was not the rambling's of a mad man. No! They were the words of a spiritual giant who was looking beyond what others could see into the future. Paul saw prophetically what would happen in the coming days to the church where Timothy was an elder. How could Timothy have known that in just a few short years after the death of Paul, the church in Ephesus would be in trouble with the Lord?

Paul saw what others did not see: the future of the church at Ephesus. Paul's heart must have grieved over this church, even as he was writing this letter to his spiritual son, Timothy. The church at Ephesus was in danger of a spiritual disaster, and they didn't know it. Timothy, Paul's son in the faith, was now a major figure in the church at Ephesus who had witnessed, firsthand, the ministries of Paul, Peter, John and James. Timothy was not a novice in the faith when Paul wrote this letter to him — he was a mature man of God who had many years of ministry under his belt.

Timothy had seen it all, done it all, and been through it all, or so he thought. It is to this now mature man of God that Paul pens these words, *"But know this,* Timothy, meditate upon what I am saying, if you don't get anything else that I have written in this letter, get this, *that in the last days perilous times will come."*

Paul's Warning to Timothy

What a sober warning this must have been to Timothy. Paul was giving, to his now mature son in the faith, a wake up call. He was telling Timothy, that if he thought things were bad. now, just wait, they are about to get worse. Paul was prophetically writing to Timothy about a day that would make the worst sinner in their day have his hair stand on end. Paul was relaying to Timothy vital information, that he had received from the Lord, about how bad things will get during these, the last days.

Paul writes Timothy about a coming day where there will be those in the church who have a form of godliness — believers who will deny the power of God, even the resurrection. According to Paul, these believers will preach a different gospel and have a different faith, even denying the one who bought them. Paul goes so far as to say, *"they will be lovers of pleasure rather than lovers of God."* In other words, their top priority in life will be having a good time. They will want to get high on life and be willing to sell their souls to do it.

Paul's warning rings out as the sobering sound of one who knows what he is talking about. I can only imagine what Paul would say if he were here today. Our moral climate is exactly what Paul predicted. We have sunk lower than the lowest of beastly desires exhibited in the days of Paul. Sin has become acceptable, Satan revered and God ignored. The devil is working overtime, knowing, his time is short. Our devious enemy has even infiltrated the church, a place of refuge for many years. We are living in the last of the last days. The words that Paul penned were more than accurate; they are a dead solid, perfect description of what we are facing today!

We should shake our heads in shame over the present state of the church! There should be an air of sobriety in our meetings. We need a serious call to repentance. We need someone to unmask the excuses that we use to cover our blatant sin — not just the sins of the flesh, but rather, the sins of the heart.

We are in real danger and don't even know it. We are straddling the fence and think that we are having fun. What is wrong with us? We are damaging something very sacred: our inner man. Our hearts, through iniquity, are being made hard, and we don't know how to stop it. We are in very real danger; we are falling into the trap that Paul envisioned when he penned this passage of scripture in the second epistle to Timothy. We are in danger of losing our first love.

Have You Lost Your First Love?

Have you lost your first love? You know, those times when you couldn't wait to meet with Jesus early in the morning. Days when all you wanted to do was spend quality time in prayer. Fasting was an easy thing for you to do. Getting to church was your top priority. In fact, you were usually the first one there. You loved prophecy, and couldn't wait to speak in tongues. You were eager to attend the midweek and Sunday morning service. The things of God were a delight to you, you constantly thought about them. Not only did you want to read the Bible, but you wanted to memorize it. The scriptures were your lifeblood. You had a passion for worship, and loved God with all your heart, soul, mind and strength.

Do you remember this time in your life? How long has it been since you have lost this, if you have lost it? Where is your heart at with God today? What are you doing to recover what you have lost; if you have lost your first love? I want you to know that we are not the only ones who have dealt with this spiritual heart disease — there have been others.

In fact, there was a whole church in the New Testament that was struggling to keep their love for Christ alive. Little did they know, they were in the fight of their lives, a fight that would determine the ultimate course of their church. These believers were in danger of losing their light for the Lord, and Jesus, out of his great love for them, was warning them about their spiritual condition. What New Testament church am I talking about? I am speaking of the church in Ephesus; they were the ones in danger of losing their first love.

The church at Ephesus was one of the top churches in Paul and Timothy's day. Everyone had heard about the church of Ephesus. In fact, many of our most relevant and useful teachings today come from Paul's epistle to Ephesus. The deeper truths of our faith are brought to life and thoroughly explained in this epistle. What does this mean to us? It means that when we think about the believers in Ephesus, we need to understand that they were not only mature in their faith; they were the epitome of Christianity in their day.

The early church looked to this church for spiritual direction. They were the center of attention for the Christian world of their day. And this, instead of keeping them on track with the Lord, literally, brought them to the point of destruction. They were in trouble with the Lord because they had lost something greater than the greatest of their teachings — their first love. Jesus, when He saw them, could only see their heart, and He was telling them, in no uncertain terms, you need to return to the foundation of your faith — not a foundation in understanding the gospel, but a vision of me, the person behind the gospel.

Jesus was longing for believers in Ephesus to once again long for Him, and this was more important to Him than the greatest of gospel truths. Jesus was more concerned with them being real, first with Him, then with themselves. This was more important to Him than anything that they might do for Him. Jesus wanted them to see how far they had fallen away from Him so that they might return to where they once had been: in total and complete, passionate love with Him.

By the time that the book of Revelation was written, we see Jesus angry with the church in Ephesus. His wrath was kindled against this church. Jesus was not only unhappy with them, but he was threatening to remove His lamp stand *(Jesus was talking about the candlestick that was giving light to the church)* from their midst. He was telling them that they were not just in danger of losing His blessing, but the church itself. Jesus wanted them to see what He saw; they had become dangerous to His work. Instead of their deeds being good for the gospel, they were, themselves, becoming enemies of the gospel, through their lack of love.

Jesus tells the church at Ephesus, ***"I know your works"*** *(Rev. 2:2)*. I see what you are doing in my name, and even though you think that you are doing the right thing in my name, let me show you what I see. Jesus starts listing their accomplishments. Talk about impressive. Most of us would be overwhelmed if Jesus came and told us that we were doing what those in Ephesus were doing. They appeared to be a church on fire. Their works were significant, especially for their day. They had all the signs of life. They had patience, perseverance, power, provision and protection. The blessing of God was upon them.

Everyone admired them and wanted to be like them. They not only didn't want anything to do with evil; they were literally out to destroy it. Talk about radical believers, they hated evil so much that they couldn't tolerate anyone claiming to be an apostle who wasn't. After all this, you would expect the Lord to say, ***"Well done, good and faithful servant"*** *(Matt. 25:21)*. Instead, Jesus tells them exactly what He sees: A church in danger of dying through a terminal spiritual disease. The Great Physician's diagnosis is critical and requires immediate attention. They are on the verge of dying through cold love, for they have lost their first love for Him.

The Danger of Cold Love

Imagine, if you will just for a second, the look that must have come across the Ephesian elders faces as they heard this prophetic word, through John the apostle. Just think about what Timothy must have thought as he received this scalding rebuke the Lord was giving to the church. Timothy must have been terrified by what he heard. It must have sent spiritual chills down his spine. I imagine that Paul's words were ringing in his ears, even as, he was hearing this rebuke from Christ Himself. Paul had warned him that they were in danger of deception, and that perilous times were coming into the world to try them. Now just a few years after the departure of Paul, they were in danger of becoming spiritually bankrupt. How could they have missed what was happening?

Sure, their prayer times weren't what they used to be when Paul was here, but they're not that bad. They must have thought we have passion for doing the work of God. Look Jesus, we spend great amounts of time seeking to do good. Our programs are the top in the country. How could you be angry with us? We are doing our very best for you, laboring to keep your gospel pure. We want what you want. We are seeking your will everyday. Somehow in the midst of all that they were doing for God they failed to see into the deep places of their own hearts — they no longer had a passion for God.

What was once extremely important to them, had now, unknowingly, taken a back seat to the work of the ministry. Somehow, in the midst of serving God, they lost their first love for God. This is how deceptive cold love can be, even among those who are mature in their faith. This is why we need to be vigilant in our defense against it.

Cold love is the Christian's nightmare. It is the most dreaded disease in the church. A church who has caught this virus is in very real danger of spiritual death. They may be doing much for God, yet going nowhere in their walk with Him. Their prayers, once the spark of revival, now may only be the burning embers of tradition. The flame of faith once burning bright, through their zeal for Christ, has now become merely the smoke of past glories. What they once esteemed as great gain, through Christ, is now but a shallow memory of what used to be. Oh, for the days of Paul and Peter; they will say. This is what they talk and think about: What used to be.

This is what the church at Ephesus was saying. They were remembering what used to be, not what could be. Their faith in Christ had been replaced by a faith in themselves. Their love for Jesus was hardly noticeable. Instead, they were known as religious fanatics and dogmatic disciples, or the frozen chosen. What a terrible place for any of us to be in as believers, and yet, this is exactly where the church in Ephesus was: The barren wasteland of cold love.

Ephesus: A Case of Cold Love

This is why the great apostle Paul was so adamant in his warnings to his spiritual son Timothy. Paul was trying to save Timothy from the potential problem that he saw in him of being led astray. Not the cold calculated evil of sinful men, but rather, the ignorant deceptions of the human heart. Paul knew that Timothy, like he, was human, and that not every attack of the enemy is outwardly visible. Paul knew that Satan could, and would, show up as an angel of light and seek to, through distraction, lead even the most elect astray — and this is what he wanted to help his son, Timothy, avoid at all costs.

Paul was looking to help Timothy avoid falling into the trap of cold love. He didn't want to see his spiritual son striving to do things for the master, without spending time with the master. Yet, in spite of Paul's fatherly wisdom and prophetic insight, it wasn't enough to keep the church at Ephesus from falling. They fell headlong into the enemy's trap — cold love.

The church at Ephesus, through their spiritual heritage, was deceived into believing that they were invincible. They did not remember that all of us, no matter how mature, is open to the attacks of the enemy. They lost their spiritual edge through spiritual pride, and as a result, received a stern rebuke and strong warning from the Lord. The Lord told them, in no uncertain terms, that unless they repented of their cold love toward Him, He would come quickly and remove His lamp stand from their midst.

I hope you can see that the church at Ephesus was in critical condition. A spiritual heart disease, cold love, had attached itself to this body, and the Lord was telling them, in no uncertain terms, get right with me or else. The church in Ephesus was in danger of being put to death, and Paul, their spiritual father, was no longer around to intercede on their behalf. The only thing that Timothy had to hold on to during this time was the memory of what Paul told him, Timothy, remember this, keep this in the forefront of your thinking, *"that in the last days perilous times will come."*

The Ephesian church was facing a crisis caused by the temptation of living in the last days, and the Lord was calling them to account not just for their actions, but their heart motives. The master refiner Himself was trying them with fire. They were on the spiritual hotseat with none other than God, Himself, asking them pointed questions about what was going on in their church. Do you see the dire straits that they were in corporately, as a church, and individually, as believers?

It is very easy for us to overlook what was actually happening in the book of Revelation. After all, the other churches listed were in much worse shape, by and large, than the Ephesian church, or so we think. In reality, God saw something quite different than what we see. He saw a heart that was no longer in love with Him, and this was of great concern to our loving Father. God knew that they could not continue on this dangerous road forever, and as a result, wanted to warn them of what lay ahead, if things did not change.

I don't know about you, but it is very easy for me to see how the Ephesian church could have thought that they were God's favorites and, as such, were exempt from his dealings. Alter all, they were the spiritual giants of their day. Paul was their spiritual father and Timothy was their pastor. It is hard for us to imagine the Lord coming to a church like this with a scalding rebuke, and yet, this is exactly what happened.

God saw the severity of their situation and sought to bring about immediate change, for their own good. God was dealing with them according to what He saw, not what they saw — and God will do the same with us. It is hard for me to imagine the Lord taking the lamp stand away from a church doing this well, and yet, this is exactly what God said that he would do, if they did not repent. And, as much as I would like to say that this story had a happy ending, it does not. Eventually the Ephesian church did die, and God did take their lamp stand away, just as He said He would.

The Ephesian church died because they lost their first love for the Savior. We would do well to look to the death of this church and realize, for ourselves, that God does not play favorites. God will deal with us righteously, according to His word and our hearts.

Overcoming Cold Love

What a terrible way to die as a church. I cannot imagine anything worse than seeing a church, that was once on fire for God, die a tragic, but avoidable death, through cold love. This is why I want you to understand that your love for God is vital to your spiritual survival. God will not tolerate churches that have a name, but do not have His life and love residing in them. Passion is a priority with God.

God wants us to be a passionate people who love Him with all our hearts. This is the first and greatest commandment given to us by God,

"Love the Lord your God with all your heart, with all your soul with all your mind and with all your strength." (Mark 12:30)

Without this passionate, intimate love in our hearts; we are in the same danger of seeing our lamp stand removed, as did, the church in Ephesus. When I take a look at the churches in the book of Revelation this one touches my heart the most. I know how frail our hearts are, and how easy it could be for us to lose focus upon what truly matters. I have taken Paul's admonition to heart. I make a conscious effort, daily, to retain my passion for God. I know that nothing in this life worthwhile comes easily, and this includes a vibrant relationship with God.

There is a price to pay to retain intimacy with the Savior. I know that unless I make a conscious effort to stay in this place of abiding intimacy with God, no matter what is going on around me, that I could fall into the same pitfall that befell the Ephesian church. And this is what I want to avoid at all costs.

If you are anything like me, you are probably asking yourself, how can I avoid falling into this satanic snare? This is why I want to give you some words of wisdom, which I have discovered, on how to avoid this trap of the enemy. Truthfully, we can avoid this snare; we do not have to become victims of cold love. God has given us some simple things that we can do to avoid falling into this trap, and for those who may have already fallen into it, I want you to know that there is a way out. This means, that no matter what is happening around us, we can be free to follow God in our hearts, if we do what Paul said to do.

The apostle Paul tells us what we need to do to avoid the perilous times that we are living in, for we are truly living in the last of the last days. We must wage an offensive war against this perilous pattern of living presented by this dark age. We cannot just sit back and expect to survive through these dark times that the enemy throws against us. We must have a plan in place that we can use to fight and defeat this foe of cold love. This is why I believe it is so important for us to understand the major warning signs caused by this spiritual disease of cold love so that we can discern the fruit of what may be a bad root in our lives.

What are the major warning signs of cold love? I believe that Paul, when he was writing to Timothy, tells us the four major warning signs of cold love and how to avoid them in our lives; they are: powerlessness, prayerlessness, ruthlessness and selfishness.

The Four Major Symptoms of Cold Love

Powerlessness

Paul was adamant in his warning to Timothy. Avoid those who *"have a form of godliness; but deny the power thereof."* Powerlessness was not a light matter with Paul. It was the first, and foremost, warning sign of a spiritual problem. Paul knew that if someone was truly walking with God, they would have power with God.

The power that Paul was talking about is more than just laying hands on the sick and seeing them recover. And, although this is a good place to start, it is not necessarily a guarantee that we have avoided the trap of cold love. We can lay hands on the sick and see them recover, give tremendously accurate prophetic words, and still be caught in the grip of cold love. There will be people on judgment day who will tell of the wondrous things they did in Jesus' name, but Jesus will say to them, *"depart from Me, you who practice lawlessness!"* (Matt. 7:23).

God does not look lightly upon those who use His name, but do not know Him: The person and power behind the name. So then, this power that Paul is talking about must be more than just doing good works in Jesus' name. Paul was seeking to teach us that we should not only have power over things, but more importantly, over our own selves. In other words, Paul was telling us that we, if we are in passionate love with God, will have the power to overcome whatever may come our way. This is the power that I believe Paul was talking about when he wrote this letter to Timothy.

Prayerlessness

Prayerlessness is the second warning sign that we have fallen into the pitfall of cold love.

How are your times with God? Are you spending time with Him? Do you enjoy the time that you spend with Him ? Is it a vital part of your life? Or could you live without it? Our devotion to God will be shown through our devotional times with Him. The time that we spend with God in the secret place of prayer does determine what is happening in our hearts and lives. Our times of prayer should be red-hot, passionate times of intimacy with God. This is why the scripture says, *"The effectual fervent prayers of the righteous avails much"* (James 5:16).

Are you fervent in prayer? When was the last lime that you couldn't go on without spending time alone with God? This should not be the exception among believers, but the norm for all believers. We need to renew our vows with God. We need to recommit our lives to Him, not just at the altar, as good as this is, but more importantly, in the prayer closet. We must enter into a secret place of prayer where we can hear and talk with God.

The church today needs some solitary confinement. We need to get away from the busyness of the world that eats away at our soul and tears our heart away from passionately loving God. We must return to the secret place of prayer. If we don't do this, then we have been forewarned in the Word of God; we are in danger of succumbing to the deadly spiritual disease of cold love.

Ruthlessness

Ruthlessness is the third sign that we have fallen into the deadly trap of cold love.

When was the last lime that you prayed for your brother or sister, even though they sinned against you? Are you holding resentment in your heart toward someone who sinned against you? Or have you betrayed the confidence and trust of someone close to you? If so, then you have fallen into the deadly grip of cold love.

The place of ruthlessness is much more dangerous than the previous two signs, for it shows that you have allowed cold love to seep into your heart. This means that you must begin applying what I am sharing with you immediately. Even if you were wronged, God warns you to repent for your wrong Allowing cold love to grow in your heart.

This is why betrayal is so serious in the sight of God. When we betray the confidence of a friend, or brother and sister in Christ, then we are in trouble with God. God will deal serious-ly with people who betray Him and those that He has placed in our life. We cannot give the Judas kiss and still expect to receive the blessing of God. And this, according to Paul and Jesus, was a major warning sign of living in the last days.

Therefore, we must not only be prepared for the possibility of betrayal, but be aware of the likelihood that it will happen to us. This is why before it does happen, we must, in our hearts, be prepared to forgive those who sin against us without reservation, no matter what has happened to us, knowing that God is mighty to defend us in these types of situations. Don't give place to the devil's cold love in your heart or life, otherwise, you may end up becoming a ruthless person living a ruthless life.

Selfishness

It is impossible, in our day, to avoid this fourth sign of cold love that Paul, when he was writing to Timothy, spoke about — we are surrounded by it everyday. Entertainment has taken precedence over spirituality, money over God. We love pleasure, and everyone is seeking to appeal to our carnal desires. It is impossible to watch television and not see this happening; from the commercial, to the sitcom; the drama, to the movie: All whet the appetite of our selfish desires. We are living in an age of selfish people.

This is why so many people avoid giving in our day. Many will avoid doing anything for others, and then, expect others to do for them. The truth is we want something for nothing, and as a result, many are not willing to pay the price that comes with loving and serving God. And this is exactly what Paul said would happen in the last days. Paul said, *"we would be lovers of pleasure, rather than lovers of God."* Doesn't this describe our society?

We are a greedy people who have an eye on Wall Street, but ignore the homeless surrounding Wall Street. Who do we think that we are deceiving? Certainly, not God. Why have we hardened our hearts and closed our minds to the voice of God? Too many people who do not want to hear what God has to say about living a selfish life. This is why so many, in blatant disregard for the Word of God, continue walking in their selfish ways. No wonder God is so close to removing His lamp stand from our land — we are closer to the Ephesian church than we think. And this, beloved, is a dangerous place to be.

Betrayal: Where Cold Love Begins

I hope that you are hearing what I am saying about the dangers of cold love. Cold love is a major sign that we are living in the last days. Cold love will be the major thing that causes believers to fall away from following Christ in the last days, according to Matthew 24:12-13, which says,

"And because lawlessness will abound the love of many will grow cold. But he who endures to the end shall be saved."

In fact, the greek word for many, used in this passage of scripture, indicates a majority of believers will succumb to this satanic web of lawlessness and cold love. The Word of God goes so far as saying that because of this pervasive attitude of cold love *"many (a majority) will be offended, will betray one another, and will hate one another" (Matt. 24:10).*

This, according to Jesus, is going to happen to a majority of believers in the last days. Members of the body of Christ will begin succumbing to this attitude of cold love in the last days, and as a result, betray one another. This is why when Jesus tells us, *"the love of many will grow cold."* He uses the greek word *agape*. Jesus is revealing to us that His love in the hearts of His people will grow cold, and as a result, many believers will lose their love for God. In others words, the church is the primary target for this attitude of cold love.

I want you to understand that these passages of scripture were written not just to those in the world, but to the church. This scripture is speaking to you and me, members of the body of Christ. The enemy, through cold love, will seek to offend us in the coming days and steal the love of God from our hearts. For this reason, we must guard our hearts with all diligence, especially during the coming days, for truly we are living in the last of the last days.

What I am sharing with you is extremely important It has the power to help you avoid falling into this deadly trap of cold love that the enemy has set for you. The truth is you can be free from the powerlessness, prayerlessness, ruthlessness and selfishness that cold love brings. You do not have to allow these things into your life. There is a way out. This is why I want you to be forewarned about the signs of cold love so that you can be forearmed to face the devices that the devil may throw against you. We must avoid, at all costs, even the slightest hint of cold love in our hearts.

We cannot practice iniquity and still expect to walk through heaven's gates on good terms. Remember what Paul said, *"in the last days perilous times will come."* We would do well to give heed to his warning, knowing, that the Lord will come upon us as a thief in the night. We do not want to be caught in a spiritual state that is displeasing to Him. We do not want to be among those "who have a form of godliness, but deny the power thereof." May God Himself deliver us from any powerlessness, prayerlessness, ruthlessness and selfishness in our lives that might hinder us at His coming.

Now that we have seen the four signs of cold love, how does cold love start? I believe that cold love starts through what we have talked about previously — covenant breaking.

This is why covenant breaking is such a serious sin in the sight of God. When we break covenant with one another, we are bringing cold love into the church. Jesus said, as a sign of his return, *"brother would betray brother,"* and parents and their children would betray one another. These are the most basic of God given covenants.

We are living in a day when there is a blatant disregard for the covenants that God has established in our lives. We do not realize what we are doing when we break covenant and betray the trust of a brother or sister, otherwise, we certainly wouldn't do it. The truth of the matter is that we are under a systematic attack by the enemy of our soul, Satan.

The devil is going around, *"seeking whom he may devour"(1 Pet. 5:8)* through covenant breaking. As such, it is vital for us to know that the enemy is the source of cold love in the church. And he is using covenant breakers to create this cold love in our hearts. For this reason, we would do well to choose our covenant partners wisely, knowing, that they may be an entrance, through which, cold love enters our lives.

Repairing the Breach
and Restoring Covenant

Making godly covenant is a matter of life and death for the church. Who we make covenant with will determine what happens in our lives. This is why I have spent so much time, in previous chapters, sharing with you how to make godly covenant. Godly covenants are important to the health of the body of Christ, for real relationships of genuine love can only happen in a place of godly covenant. This is why we need to restore an understanding of the importance of godly covenant within the church.

We were designed by God to live in godly covenant. As such, we, whether we like it or not, cannot live without being in covenant. There is no substitute in the church for believers who have learned to live in godly covenant. This, I believe, is the foundation of any and every healthy church.

Speaking as a pastor, to other pastors reading this book, we would do well to make covenant keeping a priority in our churches. Why? Because godly covenants are the lifeblood of the church.

My desire in writing this chapter on **Keeping Your First Love First** is not to condemn you, but deliver you from any cold love that may be in your heart. There is a way out! You don't have to remain trapped in this pattern of living any more. We can survive, even thrive, during the perilous limes that surround us. In order to help you do this, I want to share with you the key to overcoming cold love.

Jesus has given us the key to break free from an attitude of cold love, and it is revealed in what He shared with the church in Ephesus when He rebuked them. What is the key to breaking free from the grip of cold love? It can be summed up in one word. Repent! This is the way out of the satanic snare of cold love.

Many of us may not have heard this word in a while, but it is a word that is vital to the survival of the church. The church needs to hear this word over and over again, for revival begins with repentance. This means, that for us to experience genuine revival in our relationships, we must be willing to repent over the bad attitudes that we may have toward one another. Right now, I want to speak this liberating word to those of you who are trapped within the grip of cold love — live a repentant life.

We can overcome evil with good. Repentance is a good thing, and we need to be ready to receive this great gift from our loving Heavenly Father. What is repentance? Repentance is nothing more than a willingness to change. When we choose to turn away from the evil we are doing, to the good that God wants us to do — this is repentance. The Bible says in Acts 3:19-21,

"Repent therefore and be converted that your sins may be blotted out so that times of refreshing may come from the presence of the Lord and that he may send Jesus Christ who was preached to you before whom the heavens must receive until the times of restoration of all things which God has spoken by the mouth of all his holy prophets since the world began."

Wow! What a promise that God has given to us when we repent. God has promised us that when we repent of our attitude of cold love, He will, by His Spirit, send us times of refreshing from His presence.

Not only has God promised to send us times of refreshing from His presence, but times of restoration as well. God wants to take us way beyond renewal into restoration so that Jesus, His Son, may come again. God is calling us to keep our first love, first. To love Him for who He is, not what He can give, so that He can truly restore all that the enemy has stolen from us.

The devil, over the years, has taken much away from the church, and it is time for us to get it back. The way that God has made for this to happen is renewal. But renewal is only the beginning of restoration. Renewal restores our hearts so that we can receive God's word and ultimately be ready to receive His Son.

Acts 3:19-21 is a picture of our Heavenly Father waiting upon us to get things right so that He can send His Son, Jesus, back to us. God wants to wrap this thing up as soon as possible. He is waiting upon us to get things right: Right with Him and one another.

Covenant keeping is a serious matter, for without repentance and restoration in this area we are not ready to receive Jesus at His return.

My prayer for you is that God would restore any broken covenants He has purposed for your life, and that you would be renewed in your commitment to keep the godly covenants you are in, right now. May God help us as we wrestle through the perilous times that we daily face so that we can keep our first love first.

Chapter Four

Will You Be
My Father?

I was standing in the middle of our church sanctuary, on a cold winter Saturday night preparing for the morning service. Suddenly, a holy sense of awe filled my heart over where God had brought us, as a church, in a few short years. The Holy Spirit was filling me with an overwhelming sense of purpose and destiny, for the church I pastor. What was once just a dream, had become a reality in only a few short years. God was doing something amazing and unexplainable in our midst. He was growing a vibrant church in the middle of a spiritually bankrupt community.

We had fought many spiritual battles and gained many victories, but not without a price; it had cost us a great deal to get to this point of success as a spiritual body. We paid a great price in pursuing the vision that God had given to us, both as a church family, and myself, as a pastor. Yet now here I was, eating of the fruit of this tree that had cost so much of my time and energy. God was rewarding me for my faithfulness to Him. The promises that God had spoken to me were coming to pass, and it was exciting for me to see it happen, in just a few short years.

It was during this time, while being in an attitude of gratitude, that God was preparing me for a special blessing. God was about to use two dedicated believers to confirm His calling upon my life within my heart. Right then, while I was considering all these things, two of the elders at World Overcomers Church walked into the middle of the sanctuary. Little did I know, that they were about to ask me a question that would change the course of my life and ministry. Humbly, they both began to ask me the same question: *"Will you be my father?"*

A Passion For Fathering

Totally caught off guard by this question, I had a difficult time accepting what these two, in their innocence, were expressing, but I knew it was God. It was at this point that God began birthing within me the desire to be a spiritual father. I could tell that God, through these two elders, was calling me to a new level of authority and anointing. He was confirming His call upon me to be a spiritual father. This simple question, through sincere believers, was challenging me to move into a new direction, a direction that others had prophesied over me — spiritual fatherhood.

The Lord was moving upon my heart, and the hearts of those around me, creating a passion for what He has a passion for — fathering. Suddenly, I understood why God had brought me to this point in ministry, and my walk with Him. I could see clearly that my destiny lay beyond just building a ministry for God. I was being called by God to leave a legacy of men and women who would seek Him. God was calling me to leave an inheritance: The anointing upon my life. God was calling me into a higher standard of ministry, and as such, a higher standard of accountability.

This is why I can truly say that I stand before you as a spiritual father, knowing, through the fear of the Lord, the weight that this ministry carries.

This event has been one of the greatest turning points in my life and ministry. God has, through this simple, but profound question, sparked something deep within my heart: A burning passion to be a spiritual father. I can now see, through different Bible passages, not only the relevance, but the importance of spiritual fathers to the church.

The Bible is filled with specific references to spiritual fathers. Spiritual fathers were the foundation upon which the early church was built. During great seasons of change, spiritual fathers were the spiritual glue that held things together and brought balance to all involved. Their wisdom and dedication to Christ were the treasures of the early church.

Christ and Him crucified was their focus. This is what enabled them to steer the church in the right direction, even through stormy seasons of life. Spiritual fathers in the early church had broad shoulders, and bore, with a great sense of responsibility, the understanding that their lives and decisions were charting the future of the church.

Their primary concern was the legacy of the church, even through the cares they faced. These men willingly poured out their lives for the church. They left letters and leaders with the same heart and mind as theirs. The messages that they left, for all to see, were not just written in ink. No! They were written in the anointing of the Holy Spirit, through great sorrow and pain. It was their blood, sweat and tears that sealed the legacy of this infant church.

This was, and still is, the price that a spiritual father must be willing to pay to preserve the legacy of Christ for the church. The question is: Are we willing to pay the price necessary to be spiritual fathers in our day?

A Fresh Work of Fatherhood

Being a spiritual father is not easy; there is a great price that must be paid to walk in this glorious call. Choosing to take up the mantle of spiritual fatherhood means that we must place our lives upon the altar of Christ, freely giving Him our all.

Genuine spiritual fathers hold nothing back from Christ, and as a result, they will hold nothing back from their spiritual children.

Over the years, I have suffered greatly, sometimes at the hands of other believers. My life has truly been bought with a price, and now, through the great agony and pain that I have suffered, I realize that I am not my own — my life and ministry are God's.

Ministry, even from my childhood, was, and always has been, my dream. I have always had a deep hunger to serve God. It is this desire to serve God, more than anything else, that has enabled me to endure many nightmarish situations to see this dream come to pass. Often, my situations have often caused me to groan with words too deep to utter, as I have followed this call to be a spiritual father.

This fresh work of spiritual fatherhood that God has done in my life is far different from what many today are presenting as fatherhood. The ministry of fatherhood that I am seeking to promote is not one of lording over men, but rather, leading them, by example, to the Father, Himself. I want my spiritual sons and daughters following me, as I follow Christ — serving the Father in an unbridled simplicity. This is the example that Christ has left us.

I, as a spiritual father, desire to love, bless and train my spiritual sons and daughters through God's sufficiency in my life. I want my spiritual sons and daughters to go farther than I have in ministry. It is my desire to impart everything to them that God has imparted to me. This, I believe, is the heart of a real spiritual father, and this is what spiritual fathers are called by God to express toward their spiritual sons and daughters.

Real spiritual fathers look to give of themselves to their spiritual sons and daughters; they want their children to be blessed after them. This is why spiritual fathers make it a priority to build up their spiritual sons and daughters, not tear them down. Because this is the heart of real spiritual fathers, God will often give them tremendous spiritual gifts and authority.

Spiritual fathers will usually have greater vision and insight than those around them. Some people will often scorn or mock them because of what they see. Others will often have a difficult time seeing what spiritual fathers see, for spiritual fathers constantly look to see how their actions will affect the future of their heritage. As a result, real spiritual fathers seek to bless, and not curse, their spiritual sons and daughters.

The heart of real spiritual fathers is to establish a legacy of godly men and women who have learned how to keep covenant with God and godly covenant with others. This is why spiritual fathers are such a threat to the enemy. The devil will literally do all that he can to keep them from fulfilling God's will for their lives. Why? Because he fears the legacy of covenant keeping men and women that spiritual fathers establish through their lives.

Genuine Spiritual Fathers

Spiritual fathers are covenant keepers; they know what covenant is and what it is not. As such, they are not easily deceived by the enemy. Spiritual fathers are extremely dangerous to the devil, for they are not ignorant of his devices. Spiritual fathers, through their spiritual encounters with the forces of darkness, have learned how to spot the work of the enemy, immediately, even in seed form. The devil's tactics and temptations do not usually work on spiritual fathers, for they have developed an immunity to his devices. Often, spiritual fathers will see the enemy's plan of attack ahead of time, because they have learned how to spot his movements.

Spiritual fathers can provide formidable protection to their spiritual sons and daughters. They, through their anointing and times of prayer, establish a hedge of protection around not only themselves, but their sons and daughters.

This spiritual hedge of protection provided by spiritual fathers to all who come under their covering is like an impenetrable wall of fire to the enemy.

The enemy will often seek to turn people away from spiritual fathers. Why? Because they will lose their protection from his attacks. Often, these same individuals will blame spiritual fathers for abandoning them, when, in reality, they turned away from spiritual fathers to their own way. Spiritual fathers need to have great love for these individuals when this happens, so that, even if a prodigal son or daughter wanders off, they will, by the grace of God, be able to receive them back into the family of God, unashamedly.

The love that spiritual fathers have is not rooted in themselves, but the Father. The Father has imparted into the heart of spiritual fathers the spiritual substance of His love. God's love is not only rooted in them, it is the root of all that they do for God. This is why spiritual fathers can stand in the midst of great conflict, without fear of what others will say or do to them, and speak the word of God boldly.

The fear of man has no hold upon spiritual fathers, for the love of God within them has made them fearless. It is very often this bold fearlessness that causes spiritual fathers so much conflict, they are not afraid to call sin, sin. As a result, others will often avoid or attack them. Yet no matter what comes against them, real spiritual fathers choose to respond in love, for this is the character and nature that God has worked into them.

Spiritual fathers have been conformed by the hand of God into the image of God, and as a result, they are able to lead others into this same image, from glory to glory. This is the inheritance that spiritual fathers leave behind to those who call them father: The riches of the glory and anointing of God upon their lives. The Bible says,

"A good man leaves an inheritance to his children's children." (Prov. 13:22)

God has given fathers the responsibility to leave an inheritance for their children. God, according to the Bible, holds fathers accountable not just for what they leave to their children, but also their children's children. And if, according to the Bible, a good man leaves an inheritance to his children's children, what kind of man leaves nothing to his children?

If this is true for natural fathers, should we expect anything less from spiritual fathers? What the Bible is telling us, through this passage of scripture, is that fathers have been given what they have been given not just for themselves, but their children.

This is why God has called fathers to be good stewards over what He has given them, both in the natural and spiritual. I believe that the anointing upon spiritual fathers is not just for themselves, but it is also for their spiritual sons and daughters. God has given spiritual fathers an anointing greater than they themselves can contain. Why? So that they can deposit these spiritual gifts, graces and anointing into the lives of others.

It is this kind of ministry that pleases the Father. When God the Father sees this type of ministry being established in the earth, He rejoices, for He knows that the blessing will be passed on to the next generation. This is what I call the next generation blessing. It is a blessing that can only come from, and through, spiritual fathers.

A Restoration of Spiritual Fathers

God is holding spiritual fathers, and those called to be spiritual fathers, accountable for the inheritance they are leaving to their spiritual sons and daughters. We will have to stand before God and give account for what we have done with the spiritual sons and daughters that He has given to us. The Bible says,

"Behold, children are a heritage from the Lord." (Ps. 127:3)

and they are also a responsibility. We, as parents, are given the responsibility to make sure that they are trained in the fear and admonition of the Lord. This is the call that God has placed upon fathers, both natural and spiritual: To raise up a godly seed in the earth. God is holding fathers accountable, both natural and spiritual, for raising up covenant keeping children, children who know how to keep their covenant with God as well as godly covenants with others.

This is what we need restored in our day which has become a time of broken covenants. We need men, true fathers, pointing us in the godly way of covenant keeping. May this happen in our day as God raises up multitudes of spiritual and natural fathers.

This is the passion that God has put in my heart. The restoration of fathers. I believe that restoring fathers is a vital part of the reformation that God is bringing in our day. As we need the natural fathers of our day to take their place as the head of the home, we need spiritual fathers to take their place as the leaders of the church.

The church has been wallowing in the muck and mire of man's opinion for so long that we do not know how to get out of it. We need spiritual fathers who will pull us out of the flesh and bring us into the realm of the spirit.

The church needs to be pulled out of the carnal atmosphere that has been created by the need to entertain flesh. The church was never called to be an entertainment center, but a worship center — a place to meet with other believers, worship God and do the work of the ministry.

If this is true, how do we see these things restored to the church? I believe that the only way we will be able to recapture what the enemy has stolen from us is through the ministry of spiritual fathers.

What are spiritual fathers? Spiritual fathers are men, like David, who have a heart after God.

This is why true spiritual fathers are so concerned with the legacy of the church — they hear the heart of the Father. It is because spiritual fathers hear the heart of the Father that they want to do the will of Father, which is to establish a legacy of godly spiritual sons and daughters — to raise up children who know how to keep covenant with God and godly covenants with others. These men, like David, will even lay upon their deathbed and still be thinking about the future of the next generation. It is their sole desire to plant and establish a godly seed.

This is why spiritual fathers build their ministries around what they can give, not what they can get. Real spiritual fathers are willing to lay down their lives, sacrificing their time, to impart the heart of God to their spiritual sons and daughters. They are selfless, sacrificial servants of God who are more interested in leaving a legacy than building their own personal ministry.

Godly vs. Ungodly Spiritual Fathers

David is a perfect example of a genuine spiritual father. David spent years training his own son Solomon to take the throne. In fact, Solomon, in the first part of Proverbs, describes what David, his father, taught him. God used David to teach and impart the ways and wisdom of God to his son, Solomon. David was not only Solomon's natural father, but his spiritual father as well. God, through David, imparted supernatural wisdom to Solomon. This is something that we often overlook. It was David's teachings that put Solomon in a position to receive God's gift of wisdom.

The years of patient instruction paid off, Solomon took the way his father had paved for him. This is why when God came to Solomon in a dream and asked him what he wanted. Solomon said, *"wisdom."* Solomon took the advice of his father, David, which was to get wisdom above anything else. And because of this advice, David positioned his son, Solomon, to go farther than he himself had gone. This is what a real spiritual father is like.

Saul is a perfect example of a counterfeit spiritual father. Saul was an angry, jealous, rebellious man. Saul, even, tried to kill his own son, Jonathan. Saul spent years seeking to kill his son-in-law, David. Saul left a legacy of hatred, jealousy, murder and mistrust — this is what he passed on to his children.

Saul willfully sought to destroy his own house through jealousy. He could not stand to see his children go farther than he himself had gone. This is why when he, by the anointing, saw the future God had planned for the next generation; it infuriated him. It made him strive against the Lord, seek to kill his children, and eventually open himself up to demonic influence.

Saul went down in history as a man who at his final breath was not in the house of God, but instead, was in the house of the witch at Endor. Saul was guilty of sinning not only against himself and the Lord, but also, against his own children. Saul paved the way for the destruction of his legacy, through his own misconduct, as the king of Israel. Saul left his children a legacy of death, sorrow, despair and destruction.

The legacy of counterfeit spiritual fathers is always one of suffering and hardship. They leave to their spiritual sons and daughters a heritage of death and destruction. Their own jealousy will always abort the will of God for their own spiritual sons and daughters. Instead of leaving a blessing to their children they leave a curse.

Do you now see the difference between a genuine spiritual father and a counterfeit one?

A real spiritual father seeks to give; a counterfeit father seeks to get. A real spiritual father will look out for his children; a counterfeit father will look out for himself. A real spiritual father will watch over his legacy to protect and bless it; a counterfeit father will seek to destroy his children, fearing, what God will do through them.

A real spiritual father is one who looks to love, give and serve. They are in the business of blessing their spiritual sons and daughters. This is why real spiritual fathers make relationship such a top priority in ministry.

Counterfeit spiritual fathers, on the other hand, are looking to get. They seek to take from, lord over and compel their children to follow in their footsteps, no matter how destructive their example may be. This kind of spiritual leader is only concerned with their own ministry, not the legacy they are leaving behind, and as a result, places their ministry above any relationship.

Not Many Fathers

The church is where she is at today because we have many men who are willing to build a ministry, but few that are willing to lay down their lives to father others. Being a spiritual father is not easy; it is hard work. It is hard to work all day, making a living, and then come home, sit down and spend time with the kids. This is how hard fatherhood can be in the natural. If this is the case in the natural, how much more difficult is it in the spiritual.

Spiritual fathers not only have to be concerned about building up their ministry; they must have an eye toward the future, spending time with their spiritual sons and daughters. They must be willing to lay down their lives; Building a legacy for future ministers, not just having the outward appearance of ministering.

This is why so few, who are ministering today, take up the cause of spiritual fathering; it is hard work. They want to minister, and they want to give, but only so far. They are not willing to wholly lay down their lives to build up and bless their spiritual seed for future generations. This is the real sacrifice that is involved in being a spiritual father, and this is the primary reason why we have so few spiritual fathers in our day.

The church has not changed much in 2,000 years. The issue of spiritual fathering was one that caused Paul to groan within himself, and lament before the believers in Corinth saying, *"you do not have many fathers"* (1Cor. 4:15). This broke Paul's heart. He wasn't gloating in his own spirituality when he wrote this. No, he was grieving over the believers in Corinth, saying to himself, "who is going to take my place?"

Paul, by the Spirit, conceived this church, and he knew that it needed to be cared for by a real spiritual father. This is what Paul desired the leaders at Corinth to become. Paul was calling for men, spiritual leaders, willing to pay the price, laying down their lives, to raise up a precious spiritual seed.

As a spiritual father himself, Paul, wanted to see other spiritual fathers raised up who would continue the legacy that he, by the Spirit, had started. Paul was looking at that which was eternal; he saw beyond the veil of flesh that surrounded him. He looked beyond the temporary, that could have inundated him, to see what the Father saw: A desire for fruit to remain.

Paul wanted his spiritual sons and daughters at Corinth to go farther for God, and do more for God, than he, himself, had done. This was the heart of the apostle Paul. Paul was a spiritual father who wanted more spiritual fathers raised up so that they could go forth and help others fulfill their destiny as he had done. This, Paul believed, was the greatest need of the church in his day. If that was true then, how much more is it true today?

"My Father, My Father"

We have come to a time and place in history where we need the Elijah ministry.

The Elijah ministry is more than just prophetic ministry; it is a ministry of restoring fathers. Elijah was a man who was willing to pay the price to leave behind a heritage of faith. God was specific in His call to Elijah: *"Go and anoint Elisha in your place"* *(1 Kings 19:16)*. God, through this prophetic word, had called Elijah to father Elisha.

Elisha, at the very same time, was being called by God to be Elijah's spiritual son. God knew that Elisha was willing to lay down everything to follow Elijah, the man of God. Elisha heard the call of God, as well as the call of his spiritual father, Elijah. This call was more important to Elisha than anything, including, what he might receive from his natural parents. God, not man, was the one who had placed it in Elisha's heart to follow Elijah everywhere he went Elisha stayed with Elijah, up until the very end, when his spiritual father, was taken into heaven. Elisha, even as his spiritual father, Elijah, was being taken by the hand of God, cried out to Elijah, *"My father, my father"* *(2 Kings 2:12)*. Elisha knew his place in ministry: To be by the side of his spiritual father, Elijah.

I believe that in our day there are many Elisha's who are eagerly awaiting an Elijah to come their way. We are in the midst of a flood of fatherless Spiritual sons and daughters. There are many who want to receive a father's blessing. Many are willing to pay the price to pick up the mantle of an Elijah. These future leaders are at this very moment crying out for a spiritual father to come; someone, who will take them under their wing, and train them in the things of God. The problem in the church today is not a lack of spiritual sons and daughters, but a lack of fathers.

The church in this generation needs spiritual fathers; men who are willing to pay the price necessary to father spiritual sons and daughters. God longs to raise up these men in our day. He is looking for those who are willing to stand in the place of a father. This is the primary way that God has designed for ministry gifts and anointing to pass from generation to generation.

God wants His spiritual leaders to leave behind a godly legacy — a heritage that is holy. God the Father is crying out to men, asking them, *"Whom shall I send, And who will go for Us?"* *(Isa. 6:8)*. Who will be a father to this generation of Elisha's? God is looking for Elijah's, leaders who are willing to come and pick up the mantle of spiritual fathering. I believe that God is asking spiritual leaders today the question, *"where are my Elijah's?"*

The church desperately needs spiritual fathers who, like

Elijah, will hear the call of God, stand against the forces of darkness and pick up the mantle of fatherhood. This is the only thing that will restore the hearts of the fathers to the children so that the children's hearts might be restored to the fathers.

The lawlessness in the hearts of children is not the greatest problem that we are facing in our day. The real problem is a lack of genuine parental concern for children. We say that we care for children, and then, we leave them to their own ways and devices. This is not love; it is folly and foolishness. What we are actually doing, through our lack of concern for our children, is destroying their soul, and breeding iniquity in their hearts. Fatherlessness destroys the blessing that God desires to impart through fathers, and instead, brings a curse.

God said, that He would *"smite the earth with a curse"* *(Mal. 4:6)*, because of the sin of fatherlessness. This is why I can say, on the authority of God's Word, that what is happening in the earth today is directly tied to the hearts of fathers and their children. Not only this, I can go even farther, and say, what we see in children today is really a reflection of fathers hearts toward them. Do you see how important fathers are to the church and world?

Can you see how much we have been deceived into believing the lie that fathers are not really that important? The world would like to have us believe that fathers are just a minor part in the process of procreation. The world would like for us to believe the lie that fathers play just a minor role in parenting, and that woman have the dominant role. These are the lies the world has taught us about parenting, and the church, for the most part, has bought into these lies. We have believed that woman play a greater part in parenting, and in many cases woman have had to take on this added responsibility. Why? Because many men have removed themselves from their role as fathers and only play the role of providers.

No wonder we are where we are at today. We, as a nation, are on the edge of being smitten with a curse because men, by and large, have left their position and denied their role as fathers. This is the reason we are having so many problems in our schools today. This is why we have kids killing kids on our streets and in our schools. This is the greatest threat that the world and church is facing today: The cold hard reality of fatherlessnesss.

A Fatherless Generation

We are living in a fatherless generation; a generation that is still reeling from the effects of the industrial revolution.

The industrial revolution, although good for our economy, was devastating to the home — it fragmented the relationship between fathers and sons. The impartational nature of morality, that was passed down from fathers to sons, ceased; and a new message was sent by social scientists and now new age guru's. The chant became, "show me the money," not show me how to become a man or woman of character and integrity.

It is this singular shift in our nation that has nearly destroyed us. This shift has brought with it waves of new theories on why things have become the way they are. It is our skewed perception of reality that we need to be delivered from, and yet; many don't want to see or hear the truth that is confronting us, a truth that is calling for a dynamic change in the way we see fathers and their children.

Many want to live in the fantasy world of new age thinking that has blinded us to this truth: Father's are important to their children. This truth is something that many do not want to hear, and yet, it is this truth that has the power to save us from destruction caused by fatherlessness. May God deliver us from the ideologies and philosophies perpetuated by our own ignorance that have brought us to the brink of destruction.

It is extremely important that we realize how much damage our ideologies and philosophies have brought to the families in this nation. Children everywhere are crying out for fathers. Young girls and little boys are looking for a daddy, any daddy, to take an interest in them. These children want to come and sit on daddy's lap, but in many cases they do not know who their daddy is. We have become a warped, heartless, cruel, callused people, without natural affection, who have allowed our children to suffer greatly for our sins and moral failures.

No wonder witchcraft is at an all time high; we have allowed our children to be seduced into a way that is not good. We are the ones who have pointed them in the direction of the devil through our lack of concern for them. This is why Satanism and suicide are at an all time high among young people. According to statistics, suicide is the number one killer among young people. Is this the legacy that we are leaving our children?

What is wrong with our kids? Why are so many children going so wrong at such a young age? I believe our children recognize something that we do not. They are a fatherless generation. They are a generation struggling to come to grips with the fact that daddy is not there for them. They are lost in this world. They feel alone and abandoned by those who should have loved them — their fathers.

The statistics are staggering! According to the National Fatherhood Initiative, nearly 40% of all American children live in a house where a father is not present. This overwhelming neglect of children by fathers has led to the demise of morality among children. According to statistics, nearly 60% of rapists, 72% of adolescent murders and 70% of long term prison inmates grew up without fathers. And these are just the children, who through their conduct, we know have been damaged by not having a father.

Just imagine for a second the real story presented in the lives of countless millions not represented by this group who, nevertheless, have been damaged by fatherlessness. These are cold hard facts that tell us the real story about fatherhood in the nation of America. This is a story that few of us want to hear, and most of us would deny, were it not for these startling statistics. We are being confronted by our own sins as parents and spouses, sins which have given birth to a major epidemic in our nation: fatherlessness.

There was a father named Peter, looking to restore his relationship with his long lost son, placed an ad in a major newspaper on the east coast that said, "all is forgiven son, I love you, come home." What is so astonishing about this story? Nearly eight hundred young men showed up in response to this ad!

I wish that I could say this story was the exception rather than the rule, but I cannot. Church, there are millions of prodigal sons and daughters lost and without hope, looking for someone to call father. There is a united cry beginning to erupt from the heart of this fatherless generation, longing for a restoration of real fathers. We can have a part to play in seeing fathers restored to this fatherless generation, but first, we must identify with their pain and suffering. Only then will we be able to lift them out of it.

Fathering: Taking the Initiative

I hope that you are as concerned as I am with the state of the church and world. We have before us possibly the greatest opportunity in history: To reach and impact this nation and world for Jesus Christ.

The heart of this generation is hungry and open to the gospel of Christ. They want their world to change, and are looking for something better in life. Their hearts long for deep intimate relationships. They are looking for reality, a reality that they know can only come through real love. This is what many of them have sought to find through casual sex. Many were taught and thought that casual sex was the way to strong relationships, but, through experience, have found this to be a lie. Drugs and alcohol have not satisfied the inner craving this generation has for genuine love and acceptance.

Church, we have a message that these misguided souls are literally dying to hear; a message that we must first recapture ourselves, the message of covenant keeping. This generation is used to covenant breaking. They know the pain, sorrow and suffering caused by it in their lives. The question is: Can we be real spiritual fathers who not only know how to make covenant, but know how to keep it, and are able to teach others to do the same?

This is the calling of true spiritual fathers: To raise up a generation of covenant keepers. God is looking for bold, strong men who will be fathers to this fatherless generation. We have come to such a place, for such a time as this, to turn the heart of this generation, that is entrenched in the world of sin, back to the ways of righteousness.

This is the cry in their hearts. They are looking for someone, anyone, who will take them under their wing and lead them back to God. For many, this is the only way out of the satanic web they have become trapped in. Lost and lonely, not knowing which way to go, they have become victims of the enemies attacks, and most of them realize it. Many of them know what the counterfeit is like; this is, for the most part, all that has been presented to them.

The heart of this generation is crying out for something real;

a real relationship with a living God, and genuine men of God who will truly love and care for them. Above all else, this generation wants to find the love and acceptance that their hearts long for. They are looking for real fathers who will accept them where they are and lead them to where they are supposed to be. The question is: Are we willing to lay down our lives to become their fathers?

It takes more than just impregnating a woman to be a real father. Real fathering does not end with conception; it begins with it. God has given fathers a greater responsibility and call than we have often realized. Any man can impregnate a woman, but it takes a father to raise up mature sons and daughters.

Maturity doesn't happen by accident. This is why God has made fathering such an integral part of the family. Without a father, the family is greatly weakened, even disabled, for the father is the head of the family.

The father is what keeps the family together. He gives the family direction and purpose. This is the reason a father can have such a strong impact upon his children for good or evil. The father has been given the power by God to bless his children. He is the one who determines what children inherit.

Being a father does not end when children leave home; it often begins there. Children instinctively look to their father for wisdom, direction and purpose. God designed families to function this way, and we would do well to follow God's pattern for our families.

I hope that you have begun to see the importance of fathering. Fathering is important not just to the family, but the church.

The church is patterned after the family. Christ is the head of the church, and the church is the bride of Christ. As there are natural children born in a natural marriage, so also, there are spiritual children born through the churches marriage to Christ. When we, as the church, are connected to Christ, through an intimate relationship of prayer, spiritual children are born.

This is why Paul said that he was *"laboring in birth"* *(Gal. 4:19)* for the believers in Galatia. Paul, through effectual, fervent, birthing prayer, was fathering spiritual children in the church at Galatia. Paul, the apostle, had learned the secret to effective evangelism and discipleship, laboring in prayer. This is the reason Paul spent so much time in prayer; he wanted to see Christ formed in the lives of his spiritual children — those he had led to Christ.

Paul was a praying spiritual father who longed to see Christ formed and the will of God done in the lives of his spiritual children. Paul's prayer life, according to the Bible, had a great effect upon the churches he founded — it brought them balance and stability. Paul, through his fatherly authority in prayer and counsel, was able to steer believers away from the spiritual traps set by Satan.

The devil, in order to steer the church off course, planted devious men in the church to lead believers into legalism and licentiousness. Things became so bad in the early church, that even some spiritual leaders were deceived, through misguided beliefs, into denying the resurrection of Christ, a cornerstone of the Christian faith. The enemy, through false teaching, was seeking to deceive church leaders and believers through lies and *"destructive heresies"* (2 Pet. 2:1).

Paul spent a great deal of his time fighting against these lies and heresies. He sought to save the church from those who destroy it for material gain. Most of what Paul wrote in his letters to the church, was written in response to either specific sins believers had committed, or heresies they had adopted.

Paul was a stabilizing force for the early church through his apostolic authority. Paul was a genuine spiritual father who, in times of great danger, protected the church from those Jesus said would come *"in sheep's clothing but inwardly are ravenous wolves"* (Matt. 7:15).

The early church was filled with great spiritual fathers. They had men who spent more time leaving a legacy than building their own personal ministry. This great company of spiritual fathers united themselves as apostolic leaders for the sake of the early church, even sacrificing their lives for their spiritual sons and daughters. This is why the early church was such a strong church.

The early church was strong because there were many strong men who were willing to stand as spiritual fathers to guide it. These were not professional clergy, but practical people who lived for Christ on a daily basis. It was the strength of their prayer lives that prepared them to stand in the midst of darkness and preach truth. People came from miles around to hear them, for they knew their prayers had power to move the hand of God to heal them. These men didn't just talk about the power of God; they lived by it.

God moved mightily in the midst of the early church, because He knew that there were spiritual fathers with the wisdom necessary to bring order to what He was doing — not the carnal order of men, but the spiritual order of God. This is what the early church had, that we lack, and desperately need to get back.

The Apostolic Cry

The cry of the church should not only be for greater revelation, but for greater relationship.

We have many teachers, but we have very few fathers. This is why we think that we know the Word, but rarely do the Word. We cannot do what we have never been trained to do. This is why so many believers are wallowing around in the muck and mire of unbelief and self pity in spite of the great teaching that is all around us. The problem, for the most part, is not the things being taught, they are mostly good.

What then is the problem? The problem is that we, for the most part, have not had spiritual fathers praying for Christ to be formed in us.

Many of us have never had hands laid upon us by spiritual fathers, longing to impart a spiritual gift of God's power to us. Few of us have ever been in the classroom of a father; most of us have been in the seminary of a teacher. This is why there is so much covenant breaking in the church — we have not had many fathers teaching us how to keep our covenant with God and godly covenants with others.

Can you see why the church so desperately needs spiritual fathers raised up? We need them to see the breach in the body of Christ that has come through broken relationships; to be repaired by the power of God flowing through them and their lives.

The church is called to be a place of covenant. Covenant keeping is the life blood that gives the church it's strength and power.

Christ gave us the Lord's Supper to remind us of the covenant we have with Him and one another through His blood. We, by drinking from the cup of Christ, should not only draw us nearer to Christ, but to one another. The communion is a sign of the power of covenant, and a place to renew our commitment and desire to keep covenant.

The real communion is a place of deep abiding relationships created through a godly desire to keep covenant. This is what Christianity is all about. It is about falling deeper in love with Jesus; and through His love, falling deeper in love with others, both believers and unbelievers, alike. I believe that it is this, more than anything else, that we need in our day.

We need a divine awakening. We need a reformation in the hearts of people everywhere. We need a renewal of desire to commune with Christ and other believers by keeping covenant. The question is: How do we get there?

I believe that what the church today needs can only come through the ministry of spiritual fathers. The ministry of spiritual fathers is vitally important to the church.

Today's church needs strong men, spiritual fathers, who can point us towards Christ, unashamedly. Men who are not afraid to die for His name's sake, because they already live for His name.

This is what the early apostles did as spiritual fathers in the early church. They guided others by their example, showing Christ to all who would see or hear them. And this is what we need today, we need real apostles who have sold out to Christ, and as a result, have received the riches of heaven in an earthen vessel of human flesh.

Apostles are not freaks, strange or weird flakes. No! They are spiritual fathers to the church. They are men who, through their example, lead God's people to the inexhaustible riches of Christ. This is why an apostles eyes are so focused upon the Savior; they primarily see Him.

Christ is the center of a true apostles attention, and as a result, Christ is the center of the churches they found. Paul said it this way,

"For we do not preach ourselves, but Christ Jesus the Lord, and ourselves your bondservants for Jesus' sake...that the excellence of the power may be of God and not of us." (2 Cor. 4:5,7)

These are the words of a spiritual father, a man who is

sold out to the cause of Christ; we would do well to listen to him. This is the heart of a man called to be a genuine apostle of Christ.

The Apostolic Mandate

Being an apostle is not just a title, it is a mantle of fatherhood. Genuine apostleship is a calling to reveal Jesus to everyone at all times. A true apostle is a spiritual father who has allowed Christ to be formed in him so that he, by prayer and preaching, can form Christ in others.

Christ is the culmination of all apostolic ministry. Therefore, if the apostolic reformation taking place today in the church is to fulfill it's ultimate purpose, Christ will need to become our all in all.

God is restoring the ministry of the apostle to the church because she needs spiritual fathers. We need men who can train and equip the church to walk in the ways of Christ in a sin sick world.

The power of God in apostles overcomes the power of Satan in the world. This is why the devil hates apostolic ministry, and will do everything he can to stop it. The devil knows that there is real power in the word of a genuine apostle.

The present apostolic reformation taking shape in the church is also bringing with it a new level of God's power. What kind of power is resident in the apostolic ministry? Resurrection power, for the Bible says,

> *"And with great power the apostles gave witness of the resurrection."* (Acts 4:33)

This is what we need in our day: A healthy dose of the power of God to silence the skeptics and heretics in our midst. And this is what I believe God is doing in our day.

This is a day and hour where God is restoring truths that the church has lost over centuries and decades. The Bible calls this,

> *"times of restoration of all things, which God has spoken through the mouths of all His holy prophets."* (Acts 3:21)

God is doing a quick work to restore to us what the enemy has stolen from the church during the past 2,000 years. God is lifting the veil from our minds so that we might see clearly what the scriptures truly mean. God is giving us the spirit of revelation that is associated with genuine apostolic ministry to bring about what He has called, "times of restoration."

We are in a season of restoration, and one of the main things that God is restoring to his church, right now, is apostolic fathers.

This is what we need today, we need apostolic fathers restored to the church. In fact, I believe that this is the main restoration that must take place, for it is here, in the area of fatherhood, that we hear the Elijah call, which is a call of restoration. As Jesus said,

"Elijah is coming first, and will restore all things."
(Mark. 9:12)

So then, the Elijah call is more that just a prophetic call, as most of us have been taught. The Elijah call is also an apostolic call: A call to raise up fathers.

Why does God begin with the restoration of fathers? Because it is in the restoration of fathers that we see the restoration of families, and through the restoration of families we see the restoration of the church, and the restoration of the church brings about the restoration of all things. This is God's will for us and the way He has chosen to work with us.

God's ultimate goal is to build a covenant keeping community of believers. He will do this by restoring, rebuilding and revitalizing our relationship with Him and one another. This will happen through the apostolic ministry of natural and spiritual fathers in the church. This restoration of apostolic fathers will enable us to understand and follow by example the way of Christ and the cross, which is, the way of covenant keeping.

Chapter Five

Being Like Jesus: The Ultimate Life

O ne day, something unusual happened at one of our church services, and continued on for several weeks. This service signified a turning point in our church as the Lord began to birth through me a message that would capture many people's hearts. This message, although it had been in my spirit for years, was being held back for such a time as this.

God had been holding me back; He would not allow me to preach this word until the right time and right place. This word was a 'right now' word. It was given for such a time as this: A mighty outpouring of the Holy Spirit in our midst.

This outpouring of God's Spirit brought with it the manifest presence of God. Our church was filled with the glory of Almighty God. God knew it would take an extraordinary manifestation of His Spirit in our midst to confirm what I was saying by the Spirit.

God had chosen this day to sovereignly release this message into our body. The Holy Spirit just descended upon our church and literally took over the service. Nothing went as I had planned, as the Holy Spirit came suddenly into our church with great power and might. God wanted to do something, and He was making sure what He wanted to do would get done. Many people were healed, prophetic utterances were given and the eyes of my heart were opened. Suddenly, I saw by the Spirit the great price that Jesus paid — not just to save us, but to bring us into His very life.

I could see that Christ was crucified to bring us into the abundant life that God had prepared for mankind since the creation of the world. It was at this time and place that I caught a glimpse of Jesus and His life being the ultimate life that anyone could ever live. Immediately, I had an overwhelming desire to be like Jesus and live like Him. I, by the Spirit's revelation, had discovered the real fountain of life — *Being Like Jesus: The Ultimate Life.*

Christ's Life in You

There is no greater life available to us than the life we can find in Christ. When we come to Christ, we do not just see our sins remitted, but our spirits and souls revived. God begins working in us: Placing a seed of His own Son's own nature into our hearts. This is what Paul saw when he exclaimed to the church at Colosse,

"Christ in you, the hope of glory." (Col. 1:27)

This was Paul's revelation after a lifetime of labor for the Lord. Paul saw that it was the Father's desire to make him just like Jesus. The Father desired to conform Paul into His own Son's image so that His Son's life might be revealed through him. This almost sounds too good to be true: God wants to make His home in the house of a man's heart so that He can reveal His Son's life.

God desires to dwell in man, not just visit him, so that He can bring those who receive His Son into His Son's life. This is why Jesus said He came,

"that they may have life and that they may have it more abundantly." (John 10:10)

This was and is the purpose for God bringing His Son to earth in a house of flesh: To bring the life of His Son into the hearts of all mankind by conforming them into His Son's image. The apostle John said,

"But as many as received Him, to them He gave the right to become children of God, to those who believe in His name: who were born, not of blood, nor of the will of the flesh, nor of the will of man, but of God." (John 1:12,13)

John goes even farther and says,

"Beloved, now we are the children of God; and it has not yet been revealed what we shall be, but we know that when He is revealed, we shall be like Him, for we shall see Him as He is." (1 John 3:2)

And this is why John could exclaim, to the church through all ages,

"Behold, what manner of love the Father has bestowed on us, that we should be called children of God!" (1 John 3:1)

This is God's love: We have been born of a woman so that we might become born of God. We are sons and daughters of earthly fathers and mothers so that we might become sons and daughters of God.

When God created Adam and Eve, He made them in His image and likeness. Why? So that He might have genuine fellowship with them through an intimate covenantal relationship. Now do you see why I can say that we have been made to be in covenant with God.

Imagine, for a second, how the heart of God must have been broken by Adam and Eve's sin. This must have been devastating to the heart of God: The couple that He created to be in covenant with Him was separated from Him by their sin.

Do you see how devious the devil is? Satan, through his deceitfulness, convinced man to sin, and as a result, effectively nullified the atmosphere of covenant created by God between mankind and Himself.

When we look into the Old and New Testament, we should see God restoring mankind to Himself. The Old and New Testament paint a picture for us of God, from the beginning, seeking to restore this atmosphere of covenant relationship to man.

God, through the death, burial and resurrection of His Son, has reinstated an atmosphere of covenant to man. This is why we can enter into covenant with God and one another through Jesus: Our right to be in covenant relationships has been restored.

This is what the Bible is saying when it talks about the first and second Adam. The first Adam, according to the Bible, brought death to all by his sin. The second Adam, Jesus, according to the Scripture, brought life to all mankind through His obedience. This is why God's Word declares,

"For as in Adam all die, even so in Christ all shall be made alive." *(1 Cor. 15:22)*

In other words, *"we live because He lives."* Jesus, the second Adam, when He was raised from the dead raised man up from death into His life. This is why Jesus came: To restore His life in us by restoring our covenant relationship with The Father.

The Jesus Life

Over the years, as I have ministered around the world, I have come to realize this truth: True prosperity is not what a man possesses, but in who he becomes.

Some have patterned their lives after great philosophers and political leaders. Others after men of fame and fortune. There are many who have held their way as the highest way to the best life. Some have selflessly sacrificed their lives for the sake of their cause. Others have lived their lives to the fullest, persuading those around them of their greatness. Some have held high ideals, walked in moral integrity, and yet suffered greatly. Others have flaunted their sin, and yet, still seem to prosper. I have seen all these things in the world, yet I know for me, and anyone named by the name of Christ: There is no way other than *"the way"* and there is no life apart from *"the life"* *(John 14:6)*.

I believe with all my heart that true prosperity is being like Jesus. I have made this the number one goal for my life — I want to be like Jesus.

What, or who, are you living for? Does your life revolve around the Son of God? Are you living according to God's divine plan for your life? Until you know what you are living for, you will never be willing to die to get it. Yet, for us to be like Jesus, we must die to ourselves. We cannot continue to live our own way and still be like Him. We, those who believe in Christ, not only need to decrease, we must die. This is the only way that we will truly experience Christ's life.

It is here, in this place of death to ourselves, that true freedom and genuine liberty is found. The only place that we will ever find freedom from sin is in this place of death — death to ourselves and our own agendas.

It is impossible for Christ's life to flow through us as long as we choose to do things our own way. We cannot say, *"my kingdom come, and my will be done,"* and then expect Jesus to manifest Himself in and through us. *It isn't until we come to the point where we say to God, "Your kingdom come,"* and *"Your will be done on earth as it is in heaven" (Luke 11:2)* that Jesus comes to live His life through us. This is the only way to true prosperity, and the free gift of eternal life.

It is here, at the foot of the cross, that we enter into the purpose and plan of God for our lives, which is, to be conformed into the image of His Son, Jesus Christ. This is the ultimate goal in life — to be like Jesus.

Will the Real Jesus Please Stand Up?

Yet, for us to be like Jesus, we must see Him, not as we want Him to be, but as He is.

There are many people who have a religious version of Jesus. Jesus is hanging on their wall, but He cannot be found in their hearts. Many churches have a form of Churchianity. Their lives revolve around the church or pastor, not Christ. Many believers have replaced the Jesus revealed in the Bible with a Jesus of their own making. The Jesus they present doesn't come close to representing the real Jesus.

Some think that Jesus only did what He did in the past. Others think of Jesus, like Hollywood, the weak and wimpy, emasculated man. Some only see Jesus as a warrior, and will do anything and everything they can to defend themselves. These people religiously hold to the notion that it is their right in the kingdom of God to bear arms, and as such, are willing to go to war over this right. Some only see the good side of God, not the severe side. Some think they can go out, sin, and no matter what; still be let into heaven. Others think that if they even think about sinning, they have lost their salvation.

The church, by and large, has lost sight of what Christ really looks like, and as a result, we do not know how to live like Him. This is why we must return to the place of beginnings. We must go back and see who Jesus is, and what He did. Being like Jesus begins with the cry: *Open my eyes Lord, I want to see Jesus.*

Who is Jesus? What is He like? We need to see Jesus, for as we see Him, according to God's Word, we are ***"transformed into*** *the same image"*(2 Cor. 3:18). For this to happen, we need to hear the Father's heart and receive a revelation of His Son, Jesus. This is how we will be changed into His likeness. The Bible says,

"on this rock I will build My church, and the gates of Hell shall not prevail against it." (Matt. 16:18)

Jesus is the rock. He alone has the power to change our lives. It is this rock of revelation, seeing the person of Christ, that radically changes our lives from the inside out. This power to change is released into our lives by receiving a revelation of who Jesus really is. This is why the Bible says,

"Therefore, thus says the Lord God: behold I lay in Zion a stone for a foundation, a tried stone a precious cornerstone, a sure foundation; whoever believes will not act hastily"(Isa. 28:16). *(This can also be translated, 'will not be ashamed').*

Wow! What a source of confidence and faith Christ is to those who trust in Him. If we are building our lives upon Him, we have an assurance from God, through His Son, that our faith will not fail us. When we put our trust in Christ, the power of being in covenant with God is released into our lives. We receive not only the power to live for Him, but the ability to be changed by Him. Because of this, we can know, no matter what comes our way, we will never be put to shame, for *"all things work together for good to those who love God"* (Rom. 8:28).

No wonder the Bible tells us we do not need to fear death. Death has no power over those who believe in Christ. God has set us free from the sting of death through the death of His Son, Jesus. Christ forfeited His life so that we could have life and that more abundantly. This is why there is victory, even in the grave, for believers. We can have a strong confidence that when we shed this earthly tabernacle of flesh, we have a home awaiting us in heaven, a body made and prepared for us by the hand of God.

What a promise we have in Christ as believers! This is why we can have confidence in this life, knowing, that no one can take from us what the Father Himself, through His Son, has given to us. We can have confidence in God's promise of eternal life, for His Son's life is flowing through us. We can hear the words of Christ, ringing in our ears, saying,

"I am the resurrection and the life... He who believes in Me shall never die." (John 11:25,26)

This is why God, mocking the work of the enemy against the new creation; man or woman says,

"Death where is your sting? Grave where is your victory?" (1 Cor. 15:55)

Jesus, through His death upon the cross, has taken away the sting of death and brought us victory over the grave. This is the promise that we have in Him.

The Power of Knowing Jesus

There is great power resident in those who conform themselves into the image of Christ by the Word of God. When we take upon ourselves the image of Christ, we are transformed from something vile into an image that is beautiful beyond description, too marvelous for words. This is our right as believers.

We have the right to enter into the divine life of God. We have received from God both the divine power and promise to enter into the life of Christ on earth. God has given every believer this great privilege, no matter what our social status may be.

We are the people of the Lord, a holy nation, a chosen generation called to show forth His praise. God has given us the ability to be like Jesus — not just in secret, but before all men, no matter what.

We do not have to fear any man, because we are connected to The Man, Christ Jesus — and everything, both in heaven and earth, is subject unto Him. As the Bible says,

"God has highly exalted Him and given Him a name which is above every name, that at the name of Jesus every knee should bow, of those in heaven, and of those on earth, and of those under the earth, and that every tongue should confess that Jesus Christ is Lord, to the glory of God the Father." (Phil. 2:9-11)

No wonder Paul was able to tell his son in the faith, Timothy,

"And without controversy great is the mystery of godliness: God was manifested in the flesh, Justified in the Spirit, Seen by angels, Preached among the Gentiles, Believed on in the world, Received up in glory." (1 Tim. 3:16)

As Paul told Timothy, *"godliness (being like Jesus) with contentment is great gain"* (1 Tim. 6:6). This is the glorious power of the gospel.

There is a true story that I want to share with you illustrating the gospel's power to change men and women. There was a young man named John. John's father was a devout atheist. He was a man completely hardened to the gospel of Christ. One day John came home and asked his father, *"Daddy, can we go to church. My friends have told me that church is a place where we can meet a Father who really loves us."* John's father was furious, and said, *"No we're atheist's, and we will have nothing to do with God."*

Over many years John continued asking his dad this question, and he always received the same answer, *"No, we are atheist's, and will have nothing to do with God."* One day, while coming home from school, John was in a serious car accident. Barely holding on to life, John was taken to a nearby hospital. While in the hospital, John had a vision of Jesus standing in his hospital room. Jesus said to John, *"I love you. **Will you receive Me into your heart and life.**"* Right there, in his hospital room, John accepted Christ.

Soon after this vision of Jesus, John's father walked into the room. John said to his father, *"Daddy, why didn't you ever take me to church? I really wanted to hear about a Father who loved me. Daddy, why didn't you ever show me that you loved me?"* John continued, *"Daddy, I forgive you, and I want you to know that I just saw Jesus. He came into my hospital room and told me that He loved me. Daddy, will you accept Jesus into your life; not for me, even though I know I am about to die, but for yourself."*

With tears streaming down his father's face, John was able to lead his father to faith in Christ. Soon after, John died.

Today, John's father is now an evangelist who has ministered all over the world. This is the glorious power of the gospel of Christ.

Christ has the power to take the most hardened sinners and turn them into the greatest of saints. Jesus is able to take a father like John's, a devout atheist, a man void of love, and through the sincere heart of a son, tear down the walls of pride and prejudice.

Jesus can take a murderer, like Saul, and turn him into an apostle, like Paul. What an awesome Savior we serve! This is what God desires to do in the life of every saint. He wants to take us from where we are at to where He wants us to be. God has the power to translate us from the darkness of sin into the light of His life. The righteousness revealed through Christ's life can also be revealed in ours. This is what the gospel is all about.

The gospel shows us that we cannot do anything for God apart from Jesus. It takes Christ living in us for us to be able to live the Christian life. This *"stone of stumbling"* and *"rock of offense"* (1 Pet. 2:8) that is talked about in the Bible has kept millions of people from being like Jesus. Being like Jesus is impossible for those who do not have Jesus abiding in their hearts. This is why salvation is a vital step in becoming like Christ.

We need to be saved so that we can step into the Jesus life. The Jesus life is available to anyone and everyone who has asked Him into their lives. Yet we must not stop with salvation, as some have. No! We must press on toward the prize of the Jesus life offered for those who are the heirs of salvation. This is the first step toward living the Jesus life.

Hearing His Voice and Keeping His Word

Salvation is just the first step toward living like Christ. We, once we have made Jesus Lord of our lives, have access into something greater than many have been told. Jesus doesn't just want to take our lives, but make our lives into a living testimony of what He can do in us. We can have a life that is totally awesome!

I am a living witness of what Christ can do in someone's life. I have been around the world. I have preached the gospel to untold thousands of people. God has given me the opportunity to see thousands of people come to Christ at once. I have seen people, bound by sickness and disease to wheel chairs, rise and walk. God has allowed me to do things that were only dreams at the time. I have met people and made friends with individuals who most people only dream about meeting. God has put me in the right place at the right time so that I could receive what He wanted to give to me. Why? Because I chose to live the Jesus life.

I have made pursuing Jesus my ultimate passion in life. If you want to know what my heart beats about, it beats with a holy passion for the living Christ, Jesus. I want as much of Him as I can get in this life, and I want to have as much of His life in me as I can contain. The cry in my heart is More, Lord! More, Lord! More, Lord!

I want as much of God life in me as I can contain. I want to live life to it's fullest; not the world's way, but God's way.

We do not have to be envious of the world, or give in to the pleasures of sin for a season to have fun. We were made to live radical lives of adventure with God. We can have, and are designed to have, something far greater than just average lives. We were made to have the very life of God abiding in us. This is what the Christian life is all about it is about Jesus living in us and us living in Him. This is why Jesus said,

"If you abide in Me, and My words abide in you, you will ask what you desire, and it shall be done for you."
(John 15:7)

Jesus wants us to be fruitful people, people who are filled with His life; this is why He has called us to abide in Him. Jesus taught us,

"As the branch cannot bear fruit of itself, unless it abides in the vine, neither can you, unless you abide in Me." *(John 15:4)*

We cannot have the Jesus life apart from abiding in Christ. The Jesus life is for those who are serious about keeping the commands of God. When we keep His word, then we are showing a genuine love for the Father, Son and Spirit. If we do not keep His Word, then according to the Bible, *"the love of the Father"* (1 John 2:15) is not in us. In other words, our actions toward God, speak louder, than our words to Him. This is what the Jesus life is all about: Doing the will of the Father, by being like the Son.

Do you want to live the Jesus life? You can! Do you want to walk in victory over every power of the enemy? Do you want to see darkness scatter at your command? Do you want freedom in your finances? Your marriage? Your children? Your health? You can have all this and more!

The Jesus life is not just for the select few it is for everyone. The Jesus life is greater than any personal prosperity or success you might attain in this life. It is the highest form of life available to mankind.

The Jesus life is about you abiding in Him, and allowing Him to abide in you. God's greatest desire is not just to visit with us, but to inhabit us. We are to be His dwelling place, His home. We can be a place where God comes to take up His residence and live. God designed us, if we are believers, to be His temple. We are the temple of God. We are His home. We are to be the place of His presence.

The Jesus life is about becoming like Him by developing an intimate relationship with God. It is our relationship with the Father, Son and Spirit that will ultimately determine the quality of our life upon earth. We can have all this world's pleasure and still be void of happiness. We can be the wealthiest of individuals and still be spiritually poor. The greatest treasures in life are found in our relationships, not the earthly treasures we accumulate.

Relationship: Life's Greatest Treasure

Christ's greatest treasure was His relationship with His Father. This was His most prized possession.

Jesus delighted in the Father's love, and as a result, was willing to lay His life down for the Father. Jesus loved living in covenant with His Father. It was His covenant relationship with His Father that enabled Him to do the works of His Father. Jesus always tied what He did to His relationship with the Father. In other words, Jesus was relying upon His covenant relationship with His Father to do the works and will of His Father.

This is why Jesus could say,

"Most assuredly, I say to you he who believe in Me, the works that I do he will do also and greater works than these he will do, because I go to My Father." (John 14:12)

Jesus was showing us the power of being in covenant with the Father. He, through His relationship with the Father, was telling us that we were designed to live in covenant with the Father. This is the reason Jesus went to the cross, and was willing to die for us: To bring us into an intimate covenant relationship with His Father.

According to Christ, this is eternal life,

"that they may know You, the only true God, and Jesus Christ whom You have sent." (John 17:3)

We have been given the greatest treasure in the world: The ability to be in a covenant relationship with the Father, Son and Spirit.

I want to ask you a question: Is your relationship with God your most prized possession?

I personally have come to understand that this is the greatest gift in life. As much as I enjoy all the things God has done in my life. As much as I love my family: wife, children, parents, brothers and sisters. As much as I enjoy the church, and the wonderful things that happen in church. My most prized possession is being possessed by God. I am bought and sealed by the Spirit of God.

I love being in relationship with God. I love the presence of God. This is the greatest gift that I have ever been given. All the world's wealth can never compare to the treasures of Christ. Now, after all these years, I understand why Moses left all the treasures of Egypt — he saw the matchless treasures of Christ.

The privilege of being in covenant with God is the greatest gift ever given to man. No other treasure can compare with Jesus, God's greatest gift. Jesus truly is the reason for living — He is the ultimate life.

If our covenant relationship with God is truly our greatest treasure, how then shall we live? Living the covenant life is not always easy. There are times when we have to do spiritual labors out of dedication to our covenants. We cannot just sit by and hope that our relationship with God will grow. No! This is not how it works. We need to actively pursue God. The Bible says,

"Draw near to God and He will draw near to you."
(James 4:8)

106

And God has promised,

"And you will seek Me and find Me, when you search for Me with all your heart." (Jer. 29:13)

God will not allow us to run around in circles, for very long, if we are truly pursuing Him with our whole heart. This is why I want you to know that we can find God and know Him intimately. We don't need to be in the dark about our covenant relationship and rights with Him. We can know who we are, who God is and what He wants us to do with our lives. Jesus came to bring us clarity about life. We are called to live lives of purpose, not lives of confusion.

Entering Into Your Destiny

Covenant people are people of purpose and destiny.
The Bible tells us,

"walk circumspectly, not as fools but as wise, redeeming the time, because the days are evil." (Eph. 5:15,16)

God wants us, through His wisdom, to reverse the curse in the earth by living in covenant with Him. This is the call upon every person who names the name of Christ. We can be different. We don't have to walk in the ways of this world. We can look sharp, pay our bills on time, have the best in life and still have an intimate covenant relationship with God.

Because God wants us to,

"prosper in all things and be in health, just as your soul prospers." (3 John 2)

We are called to prosper in life so that we can prosper in our relationship with God. We need to change our stinking thinking about the blessing of being in covenant with God. We need to put on the mind of Christ. We need to become covenant minded, and learn how to walk in an intimate covenant relationship with God. The question is: Are we ready to lay aside our preconceived notions about who God is and what He will do in our lives?

We must be willing to change. Change positions us, through the covenant that we have with God, for His blessing to flow into and through our lives. God has called us to be blessed so that we can be a blessing.

We have been called by God to be a blessing to those around us. As we learn how to be a blessing to those around us, we can be all that God created us to be. We are designed by God to be a blessing not only to other people, but to God Himself. This is how we develop an intimate covenant relationship with God and others: By learning how to be a blessing. We can be like Jesus, and live our lives for the Father as He did.

God wants us to have an abundant life through Christ. This is why I want to share 10 principles that will help us walk in a deeper covenantal relationship with God. I believe that if we apply these things in our lives, we will wake up more like Jesus, everyday. People may even stop us on the street and tell us how much we remind them of Jesus. We may be sitting in a restaurant, and suddenly, people around us will start talking about Jesus. These 10 principles will totally revolutionize our lives, causing us to carry the very life of Jesus to those around us.

10 Principles for Being Like Jesus

1	Living in God's presence.
2	Finding the heart of God.
3	Walking in the heart of God.
4	Thinking like God thinks.
5	Talking like God talks.
6	Mimicking what God does.
7	Following God all the time.
8	Staying connected to God.
9	Serving God everywhere.
10	Decreasing more everyday.

These 10 principles may sound simple, but they can, at times, be very hard to daily walk in. These principles are powerful practical steps that we can use to live life like Jesus.

We were made to live like Jesus. Any believer, who seriously takes these principles to heart, is qualified to live like Jesus. We were all made to be like Him. We do not need to be a pastor, prophet or apostle to be like Jesus. We do not need to be rich or famous to be like Jesus. Every believer who has a sincere desire to follow Christ is able to live and walk in the shoes of Jesus.

We can follow in His footsteps, and do His will, because He followed in His Father's footsteps, and did His Father's will. We have the greatest privilege ever given to man: *"To live and move and have our being in Him"* (Acts 17:28). This is what being like Jesus is all about walking in the ways and will of our Father, God.

Living in God's presence.

Where do we start? I believe that we must start at the place of beginnings — the presence of God. We must, in our hearts, yearn for the presence of God, in such a way, that nothing hinders us from entering into it.

Living in God's presence is the greatest thing in life. Truly, there is fullness of joy in the presence of God. This is why Jesus is so joyful and full of life. We, too, should be filled with the joy of our Father in heaven. The Bible tells us to,

> *"Rejoice always, and in everything give thanks; for this is the will of God in Christ Jesus for you."*
> *(1 Thes. 5:16,18)*

so that we can abide in God's presence always.

Finding the heart of God.

It is only as we abide in the presence of God that we start to hear and understand the heart of God. Finding the heart of God is vital to our spiritual survival.

The enemy has always sought to twist our understanding of God. The devil knows that if he can warp our view of God that he can hinder us from following God. This is why the enemy is so intent on destroying our understanding of the Father's heart — he wants to keep us ignorant of what the Father is really like.

Because of this, we need to recapture what the Father is really like. We must see the Father as He is in the face of Jesus, for he that has seen Jesus, has seen the Father. It is my prayer that God would give us a fresh glimpse of His Son so that we might see and understand the Father's heart.

Walking in the heart of God.

Once we see and understand the Father's heart; we are responsible for walking in what we have learned. It is not enough to know that our Father loves us. We must; through His love, love others. This is the essence of the Father's heart. Expressing the fullness of His love to those around us.

It is impossible for those who genuinely desire to be like Jesus to know the Father's heart and then not walk in it. This is why Jesus said,

"If anyone loves Me, he will keep My word... He who does not love Me does not keep My words." *(John 14:23,24)*

It is by our obedience that we demonstrate our love to God. We can say that we love God, but when we hear Him, if we do not obey Him, then we are lying to ourselves, and not expressing a genuine love for God.

Thinking like God thinks.

This is the way that God thinks. When we start to think like He thinks, then we will begin to do what He does. This is why finding what God is thinking about situations, that we are facing, is critical to our ability to walk in covenant. This means, for us to walk in genuine covenantal relationship, we must keep our minds focused upon things from heaven's perspective, rather than maintaining an earthly mindset.

We must not let the enemy deceive us. We cannot flirt with the world, and still be the friend of God.

The Bible says,

"Come out from among them and be separate, says the Lord." *(2 Cor. 6:17)*

We will do ourselves a great deal of good if we pay attention to this warning, for it is straight from the mouth of God.

Talking like God talks.

When we in our hearts begin to think like God thinks, then we will start talking like He talks. We cannot talk like God if we are not thinking like Him,

"For out of the abundance of the heart the mouth speaks." *(Matt. 12:34)*

Have you ever stopped to listen to what was coming out of your mouth? Were you shocked by what you heard? This is why it is so important to watch what is coming out of our mouths, for it reveals what is truly in our hearts.

We cannot have a heart like God's, and then talk like the world. Those who are of the world talk about worldly things. Those who are of God hear and talk about the words of God. This is the truth, and it has the power to set us free from worldly things, if we walk in it.

Mimicking what God does.

Children will often seek to imitate their father. I want to ask you a question: When was the last time that you did what you saw your Father doing?

We cannot be good children of God if we are not looking to imitate Him. The Bible tells us that we need to **"Study to show ourselves approved unto God"** *(2 Tim. 2:15)*, so that we can learn how to mimic God.

Mimicking God is not mocking Him. Mimicking God is the greatest compliment that we can pay God in front of the world. When we do what we see our Father doing, then we are bringing glory to Him, and this, above all else, pleases Him. Not only does this please Him, but it brings glory and honor to His name, and it enables us to learn how to live for Him in this present world.

Following God all the time.

We can only live for God to the degree that we follow Him. This is why we need to be sensitive to the Holy Spirit's work in our lives at all times and in every situation. When the Holy Spirit tells us to do something, we need to learn to do it without hesitation. It is this kind of obedient attitude that enables us to follow God even when things aren't going well. We will be able to keep ourselves together and our spiritual lives in gear, even if, things start falling apart. Then God will deliver us from the difficult circumstances we are facing, because we are keeping our heart in tune with His heart.

Having our heart tuned to the heart of God is what connects us to God, and keeps us under His protection.

Staying connected to God.

Staying connected to God, through the mystery of covenant, is vital to living like Jesus. Without this connection to Christ, we have no guarantee of protection by Him, and as such, are open to the enemy's attacks.

Our enemy hates it when we stay connected to God at all times, by His Spirit, for it overthrows the devil's plans against us. When we live in constant connection with God, we live in a complete state of protection from our enemy, Satan.

We need God to protect us from the enemy's attacks so that we can enter into the Jesus life. Without this protection through connection that comes from God, it is impossible to serve Him effectively.

Serving God everywhere.

We are called to be the servants of God at all times, everywhere. This is how we, as believers, enter into our destiny.

Our destiny in God is determined by the way we serve Him. If we serve God faithfully, then He will promote us. The Bible says,

> *"He that is faithful in what is least is faithful also in much."* *(Luke 16:10)*

When we faithfully serve God with what we have, then God will give us more. This is how we increase in Christian character and develop a deeper walk with God, such that, we delve into the riches of our purpose and destiny in Christ. And isn't this what we want?

Decreasing more everyday.

It should be our desire and prayer to serve God — He has done so much for us. Yet we can only serve God, to the fullest extent of our ability, when,

"it is no longer I who live, but Christ lives in me."
(Gal. 2:20)

As John the Baptist said,

"He must increase, but I must decrease." *(John 3:30)*

It is only as we decrease that Christ can be exalted and magnified in us. This is why we need to allow the Holy Spirit to take us to the cross, so that we might say, like Paul, *"I die daily"* *(1 Cor. 15:31)*. It is through this daily death experience that we experience the life of Christ This is where real life is found: As we decrease and He increases.

Becoming Who God Called You to Be

God has a special call that He has placed upon you. No one can do what you can. You are an important person in the sight of God, and a vital part to the plan of God for this generation.

There are no extraordinary believers, only ordinary believers who serve an extraordinary God. You are God's chosen vessel. You are God's man or woman of faith and power.You can be, and were designed to be, all that God created you to be. There should be no area of lack in your life. You should have everything you need to fulfill your calling. The Lord has provided more than enough for us. We all have the ability to receive more than enough to fulfill God's will for our lives.

I want you to know that no matter what has happened in your life, no matter what sin you may have committed, or problems that you may have encountered, there is enough spiritual strength and stamina in you to overcome and win the race that has been set before you. God has designed you to live in total and complete victory — you were built to be a victorious overcomer in this life.

God has placed an ability in every believer to be an overcomer. Every believer has enough of Christ in them to become a World Overcomer, for Christ has overcome the world. This means that we can live in a constant state of victory, for Jesus, the victor, lives in us.

God has made us a victorious army of believers in Christ. We are called to be in the great army of God. How do we sign up and join this great army of believers? By laying aside anything and everything that hinders us from following God's purpose for our lives. We have a promise from God, that clearly states, we have been called into God's victorious overcoming army.

Don't allow the devil to steal your place of promise from you. You can enter into the fullness of the promises given to those who overcome.

Jesus wants you to overcome so that you can receive what He died to give. The price that Christ paid is enough for you, me and anyone who truly wants to live in victory over every enemy. This is God's will!

It is not God's will for us to struggle and suffer all the way through life. The trials we experience should refine us and bring us into a place of greater faith in God. When we are going through a trial, we should be able to say, *"God delivered me from that situation, and I know that He will deliver me from this situation, but even if He doesn't, I will never bow my knee to you, devil!"* These are the words of a person who is strong and knows their God.

This kind of person has become a winner over the adversities of life. When life comes against us, this is what we must learn to say. When the winds of adversity blow our way, we should be able to stand strong and say, *"No! I'm not moving not one bit. I am going to stand and see the salvation of God."* These are the words of a person who is on their way to becoming all that God created them to be.

God, in our day, is restoring a radical, revolutionary remnant of believers. The Holy Spirit is drawing believers everywhere into this holy remnant. God is calling for men and women who are willing to do whatever it takes to follow Him.

We can be a part of this remnant. Our churches should be filled with sold out, committed, radical people who are willing to do whatever it takes to win the fight of faith. Christ is calling us into this kind of commitment as believers. We are being called into the radical realm of real zeal, for this is where we find Jesus.

Jesus was and is a zealous person. It was His zeal for the house of God that caused the leaders of His day to want to crucify Him. The zeal of God consumed Him and caused His life to be a holy flame unto the Father. Jesus was consumed with a holy passion to see the kingdom of God come, Gods way.

Jesus did not settle for anything less than His Father's will. The last breath that Jesus took shows us how much He was willing to pay to do the Father's will. The question is: Are we willing to pay the price that it will take for us to do the Father's will?

Crying Out, Coming Home, Keeping Covenant

I believe that there is a holy cry arising, that can be heard across the nations. There is a holy dissatisfaction for the things of the world entering into the hearts of men, women, boys and girls. This thunderous cry is the result of the brokenness so many have experienced through covenants that have not been kept.

We have fallen onto the path of broken covenants. We have become a people, church and nation of covenant breakers. We have slipped into the sin of breaking fellowship with God and one another. The time has come when we as a nation must return to the Lord.

We must find our first love for Christ again. I believe that this is the reason why there are so many songs being written today seeking to revive our first love. God Himself is orchestrating a united cry within our hearts: *"Change me O Lord, yesterday's gone, today I'm in need, Holy Ghost fire fall on me, Holy Ghost power breathe on me, Holy Ghost shower rain on me."*

This is the cry of the radical, revolutionary remnant that God is raising up. May this become our cry, during the coming days, as we seek to build long-lasting relationships by keeping covenant with God and our godly covenants with others.

So, be encouraged, because challenge brings change and change breaks chains. For one can still put a thousand to flight and two, ten thousand!

A Word From Jesus
A Loving Reminder to My Church

If you are where you are supposed to be, you will hear what you are supposed to hear.

If you are where you are supposed to be, you will have what you are supposed to have.

If you do what you are supposed to do, you will have what you are supposed to have.

Some could not, but others would not.

He who has ears, let him hear what I am saying to My church.

If you cannot hear, you cannot follow. If you cannot follow, you are lost.

Position yourself! Position yourself!

I give no special invitations, and I will manifest without warning!

Whosoever will, may come.

Are you ready for My fullness?

Are you ready to be completely restored?

Are you ready for the glorious rapture?

My sheep hear My voice, and follow Me. Run to Me and to My house, and watch and see what I will do!

Do you love Me, do you really love Me? Behold, I come quickly!

Jesus

A Covenant Prayer

Dear Heavenly Father,
I come to You in the mighty name of Your Son, Jesus Christ. I
thank You for sending Him to the cross in my place. I thank You
for the covenant that He made for me through His shed blood.

God, please search my heart. If I have broken any covenant
against Your will, I ask You to forgive me. As I make things right
with You, I will be certain to do the same with anyone in whom
I am needing to make matters right with.

Father, I ask You for wisdom, grace, boldness, humility, and
most of all, compassion. I will be a covenant person. I thank
You for restoring me. I thank You for challenging and changing
me. I allow You to be my first love, now and always.

For further information regarding books and tapes by Jim DiPalma, or to schedule him for a speaking engagement at your church or conference, you may contact him at:

WORLD OVERCOMERS CHURCH
990 N. County Farm Road
Carol Stream, IL 60188
Phone: (630) 588-9999
Fax: (630) 588-0999
E-mail: woc1@excite.com